ADDISON-WESLEY

QUEST 2000

EXPLORING MATHEMATICS

Randall I. Charles   David C. Brummett   Ricki Wortzman
Lalie Harcourt   Carne S. Barnett   Brendan Kelly

Addison-Wesley Publishing Company

Menlo Park, California • Reading, Massachusetts • New York
Don Mills, Ontario • Wokingham, England • Amsterdam • Bonn
Paris • Milan • Madrid • Sydney • Singapore • Tokyo
Seoul • Taipei • Mexico City • San Juan

The Professional Team

Contributing Authors
Elisabeth Javor, Los Angeles, California
Alma Ramirez, Oakland, California
Freddie Lee Renfro, Bay Town, Texas
Mary M. Soniat-Thompson, New Orleans, Louisiana

Multicultural Advisors
Barbara Fong, Atherton, California
Jeanette Haseyama, San Diego, California
James Hopkins, Seattle, Washington
Lyn Tejada Mora, San Diego, California
Glenna Yee, Oakland, California
Teresa Walter, Encinitas, California
Roger E. W-B Olsen, San Francisco, California

Technology Advisors
Cynthia Dunham, Framingham, Massachusetts
Diana Nunnaley, Maynard, Massachusetts
Fred Crouse, Centreville, Nova Scotia
Flick Douglas, North York, Ontario
Susan Siedman, Toronto, Ontario
Evelyn Woldman, Framingham, Massachusetts

Editorial Coordination: McClanahan & Company

Design: McClanahan & Company

Cover Design: The Pushpin Group

ISBN: 0-201-84003-0

4 5 6 7 8 9 10 - VH - 99 98 97 96

Table of Contents

Unit 1: Collecting and Analyzing Data

Launch	What patterns can we see in data?	vi–1
Activity 1	Information, Please	2–3
Activity 2	From Movies to Shoes	4–6
Activity 3	A Piece-ful Day	7
Activity 4	Prime Time for Cartoons	8
Activity 5	Tour Time!	9–11
	People, Society, and Mathematics: Hand-y Representation	12
Activity 6	Time on Your Hands	13
Activity 7	Fold a Flake	14–15
Culminating Work	Gathering Data for a Pen Pal Class	16–17

Unit 2: Representing Numbers

Launch	How can we show numbers?	18–19
Activity 1	What's in a Name?	20–21
Activity 2	So Many Words!	22–23
Activity 3	Build the Greater Number Game	24–25
Activity 4	Super Swamp Thing	26–27
	People, Society, and Mathematics: Counting With Wolves	28–29
Activity 5	Straightshooter	30–32
Activity 6	Be a Winner	33
Culminating Work	Showing Large Numbers	34–35

Unit 3: Combining, Comparing, and Separating

Launch	What are addition and subtraction?	36–37
Activity 1	Legs in the Barnyard	38–39
Activity 2	Side by Side	40–41
Activity 3	Home on the Range	42–43
Activity 4	Problems, Problems, Problems	44–45
Activity 5	Closing In On 1,000	46–47
	People, Society, and Mathematics: The Case of the Missing Arrow	48
Activity 6	Big Hand	49
Activity 7	Take it Away!	50–51
Activity 8	When is an Estimate Enough?	52–53
Activity 9	Munchy Meals at Mike's	54–55
Culminating Work	Pet Care Costs	56–57

Unit 4: Locating and Mapping

Launch	How can we make and use maps?	58–59
Activity 1	Know Your Place!	60–61
Activity 2	Map That Picture	62–63
	People, Society, and Mathematics: Sea Shell Maps	64
Activity 3	Getting from Here to There	65–66
Activity 4	Where Is It?	67
Activity 5	Dinosaur Discovery	68–69
Culminating Work	Making Maps	70–71

Unit 5: Grouping and Sharing

Launch	How can we use equal groups?	72–73
Activity 1	Twice as Nice	74
Activity 2	Up to 100!	75–76
Activity 3	The Cost of Stamps	77–78
Activity 4	Quilt Patterns	79–80
	People, Society, and Mathematics: Are You Game?	81
Activity 5	The Array Game	82–83
Activity 6	Collecting Coins	84–85
Activity 7	Fair Shares	86–87
Activity 8	Showing Division	88–89
Activity 9	What's the Question?	90–91
Activity 10	The Land on "0" Game	92–93
Culminating Work	Design Your Own Stamp Booklet	94–95

Unit 6: Counting and Exchanging Money

Launch	How can we use money?	96–97
Activity 1	Using Vending Machines	98–99
Activity 2	Mouthwatering Menus	100–102
	People, Society, and Mathematics: Cowrie Shell Money	103
Culminating Work	Currency Exchange	104–105

Unit 7: Exploring Length And Area

Launch	How can we measure length and area?	106–107
Activity 1	A Banquet!	108
Activity 2	How long is your arm span?	109–110
Activity 3	Are you a rectangle or a square?	111
Activity 4	A Hand-Some Picture	112–113
Activity 5	Different Shapes, Same Area?	114
	People, Society, and Mathematics: At Arm's Length	115
Activity 6	The Big Coverup	116–117
Activity 7	When Is an Estimate Good Enough?	118–119
Culminating Work	Have a Measuring Olympics	120–121

Unit 8: Describing Parts and Wholes

Launch   How can we describe parts of wholes?............122–123
Activity 1   Make it Fair!.................................... 124
Activity 2   Covering Up................................ 125–127
Activity 3   Going Halves 128
               People, Society, and Mathematics:
               Look to the Trees 129
Activity 4   Fold and Fold Again...........................130
Activity 5   Fraction Reaction 131
Activity 6   A Good Diet............................... 132–133
Culminating Work   Making Matches......................... 134–135

Unit 9: Exploring Symmetry

Launch   How do we know it has symmetry? 136–137
Activity 1   Find the Line! 138–140
Activity 2   Halve a Heart 141–143
               People, Society, and Mathematics:
               Repeat Yourself 144
Activity 3   Symmetric Designs Plus..................... 145–147
Culminating Work   Puzzling Steps............................ 148–149

Unit 10: Building Arrays

Launch   How can we multiply using arrays? 150–151
Activity 1   Photo Finish 152
Activity 2   Ways with Arrays........................... 153–154
Activity 3   Solve a Simpler Problem 155–156
Activity 4   Missing Sides 157–158
Activity 5   Making Arrangements....................... 159–161
               People, Society, and Mathematics:
               Doubles or Lattice Work?..................... 162–163
Activity 6   Telling Times............................... 164–165
Culminating Work   Make a Party Planning Guide.................166–167

Unit 11: Exploring Chance

Launch   What are the chances?........................168–169
Activity 1   What Are the Chances? 170–171
Activity 2   It's Certainly Impossible......................172–173
Activity 3   Chances Are 174–176
               People, Society, and Mathematics:
               What are the Chances of Landing
               in South America?.............................177
Activity 4   The Probability Game........................178–179
Culminating Work   Making a Game of Your Own 180–181

$\mathscr{W}$hat patterns can we see in data?

Information, Please

Think about these questions:

What's your favorite video?

What's your shoe size?

How many hours do you sleep at night?

How long does it take you to get to school?

AMAZING
F A C T S

The biggest feet known are those of Haji Mohammed Alam Channa of Pakistan who wears size 22 sandals.

If you and 5,873 of your best friends wanted to go out to a show, you could all fit in Radio City Music Hall in New York City. It seats 5,874 people.

One of the most famous characters in American literature is Rip Van Winkle. According to the story he slept in the mountains for 20 years.

George Meegan from Great Britain walked 19,019 miles from the southern tip of South America to Northern Alaska. It took him 2,426 days.

Rick Hansen wheeled his wheelchair over 24,900 miles through four continents and 34 countries. He left Vancouver, British Columbia on March 21, 1985 and arrived back there on May 22, 1987.

The longest regularly scheduled bus route in the United States is between Miami, Florida and Los Angeles, California. The route is 2,642 miles and takes 61 hours and 45 minutes.

From Movies to Shoes

These graphs show data for some of the questions you worked on.

Compare your class graph with the graph shown.

1.

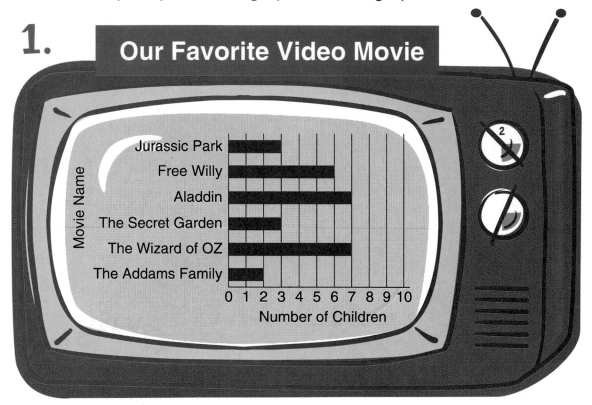

Our Favorite Video Movie

Movie Name

Jurassic Park
Free Willy
Aladdin
The Secret Garden
The Wizard of OZ
The Addams Family

0 1 2 3 4 5 6 7 8 9 10
Number of Children

2.

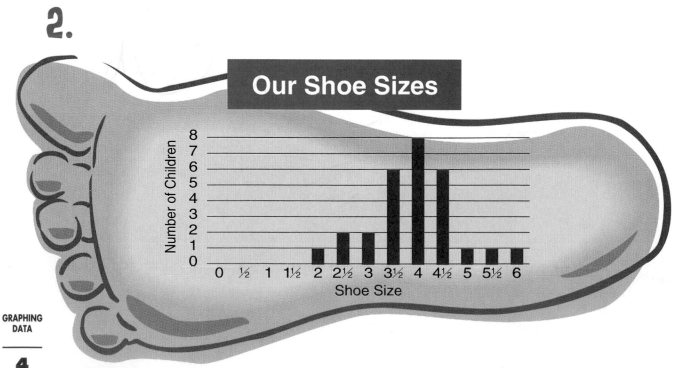

Our Shoe Sizes

Number of Children

8
7
6
5
4
3
2
1
0

0 ½ 1 1½ 2 2½ 3 3½ 4 4½ 5 5½ 6
Shoe Size

3.

How Many Hours We Sleep at Night

4.

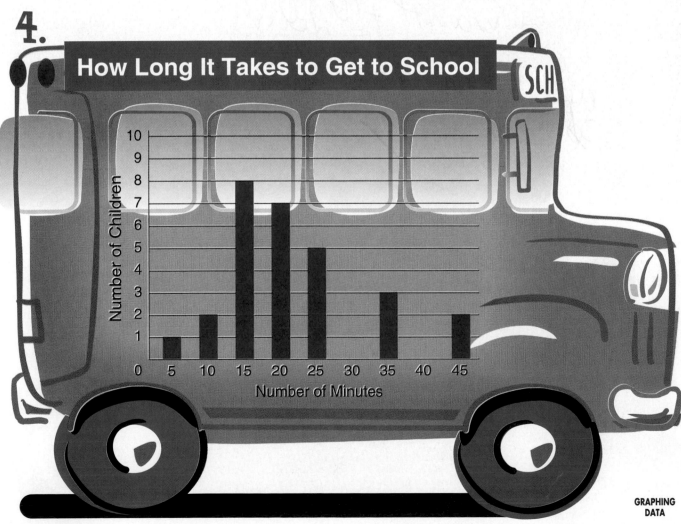

How Long It Takes to Get to School

ON
YOUR
OWN

Look at this table. Then make a bar graph and answer the questions.

Runner	Seconds to complete 50 yard dash
Ben	10
Jake	12
Owen	13
Paul	10
Fran	14
Fred	12
Gordon	13
Janelle	15
Elise	13
Kim	11
Onika	11
Zoë	10
Mei	13
Yolanda	14

1. Did Ben run faster or slower than Jake? Explain.

2. Is this statement true or false? Explain.
All children finished in 15 seconds or less.

3. Was there a winner? Explain.

4. Write three statements about your graph.

5. *My Journal:* Which graph in this activity was the most interesting to you? Explain.

A Piece-ful Day

The inspector of buckets at the Power Polygons factory needs your help. She needs to do a quality check and has asked if your class set of Power Polygons is complete and has the correct number of each shape. How could you find out?

▶ Two Ways to Record Your Data

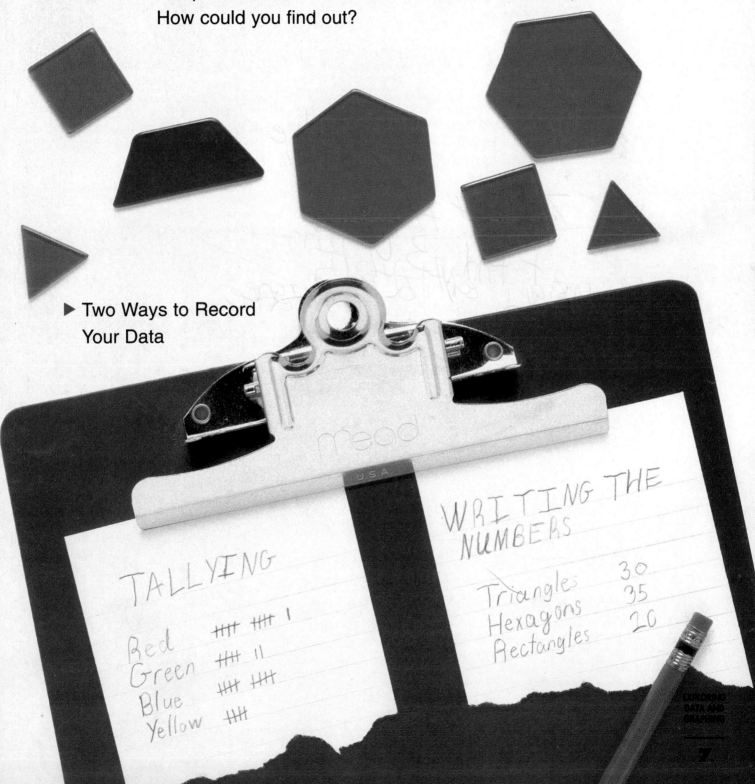

TALLYING

Red   ⊬⊬⊬ ⊬⊬⊬ I
Green   ⊬⊬⊬ II
Blue   ⊬⊬⊬ ⊬⊬⊬
Yellow   ⊬⊬⊬

WRITING THE NUMBERS

Triangles   30
Hexagons   35
Rectangles   20

Peak Time for Cartoons

Saturday morning is peak time for cartoons.

How many minutes long is the longest cartoon program?

How many minutes long is the shortest cartoon program?

What length show is most common during Saturday morning cartoon prime time?

Organize your data any way you choose. Write and tell what you discovered.

Would you expect to find the same length and type shows on Saturday night from 7 p.m. to 11 p.m.? Explain.

SATURDAY NOV. 20 — MORNING

	7:00	7:30	8:00	8:30	9:00	9:30	10:00	10:30
2	Scratch	Nick News	Marsupllam: (cc)	The Little Mermaid	Garfield & Friends		All New Dennis	Teenage Turtles (cc)
5	World in 80 Dreams	Hurricanes	Dog City	Droopy Detective	Bobby's World	Eekl & Thunderlizar	Tiny Toon Adventures	Taz Mania (cc)
7	The Mad Scientist Toon Club		Cro (cc)	Wild West O. O. W.	Sonic the Hedgehog	The Addams Family	From the Cryptkeeper	The Bugs Bunny Show
11	Paid Programming				News Closeup	Best Talk	Bill Nye Science Guy	Energy Express
41	Programa Comprado	Programa Comprado	Programa Comprado	Programa Comprado	T.V. O		Carrusel las Americas	

SATURDAY NOV. 20 — PRIME TIME

	7:00	7:30	8:00	8:30	9:00	9:30	10:00	10:30
2	News	Hard Copy (cc)	Dr Quinn, Medicine Woman				Walker, Texas Ranger (cc)	
5	Roseanne: Crystal is obsessed with her late husband.	Inside Edition Weekend (cc)	Cops: New York Transit Authority Police patrol subways	Cops: Briefing on drug warrants	Front Page (cc)		News	
7	News	Views	George: Tenant offers George a challenge.	Where I Live: The kids are growing up too fast	The Paula Poundstone Show (cc)		The Commish: A would-be suitor is obsessed with Cyd; Tony learns a startling fact in the case of elderly female banker	
11	Star Trek: The Next Generation: Force of Nature. (cc)		MOVIE : THE RED STONE (G, '83) ★★ A documentary on Ayers Rock				News (cc)	
41	Sabado Gigante							

Tour Time!

- All tours meet at the Ranger Center at Timberlake Park.

- Wear suitable clothing. Bring sunscreen.

- Arrive 10 minutes BEFORE the tour begins to sign up.

TOUR	Leaves at—	Returns by—
Bike Hike Around the Lake (trail bikes available)	8:30 a.m. 4:00 p.m.	11:00 a.m. 6:15 p.m.
Bird Watch	7:30 a.m.	8:30 a.m.
Canoe Trip and Island Picnic	10:30 a.m.	3:45 p.m.
Cave Adventure	1:00 p.m.	3:20 p.m.
Cliff Trail Hike (must be 13 or older)	9:00 a.m. 2:30 p.m.	11:30 a.m. 5:00 p.m.
Exploring Ruins	11:00 a.m. 2:30 p.m.	12:30 p.m. 4:30 p.m.
Kids' Crafts (for ages 5-7) (for ages 8-10)	10:15 a.m. 1:30 p.m.	11:15 a.m. 2:45 p.m.
Nature's Picnic	12:15 p.m.	1:30 p.m.
Riverbank Horseback Ride	8:15 a.m. 2:15 p.m.	10:00 a.m. 4:00 p.m.
Wetlands Walk	8:15 a.m. 3:00 p.m.	9:00 a.m. 4:25 p.m.
Wild Berry Picking	1:40 p.m.	2:45 p.m.
Wildflower Walk	10:45 a.m. 12:40 p.m.	11:25 a.m. 1:20 p.m.

Solve these problems with your partner.

1. Which is the longest tour at Timberlake Park? How long does it last? Which is the shortest tour? How long does it last? Compare the lengths of these tours.

2. If you take the afternoon Wetlands Walk, how long will you be gone?

3. You live 40 minutes from the park. What time should you leave your house to get to the park in time to sign up for your favorite tour? If you left right after the tour ended, what time would you get home? Explain your thinking.

4. You have time for a tour that lasts $1\frac{1}{2}$ to 2 hours. What choices do you have?

5. You arrive at the park at 10:50 a.m. What is the earliest tour you can sign up for? Explain.

6. You want to do two tours. You want at least a half-hour between tours, but not more than an hour. Which tours can you choose? How long will each tour last?

7. You want to take a tour that ends in time for you to meet a friend at 12:30 p.m. Which tour will you pick? How long is it from the end of the tour to 12:30 p.m.?

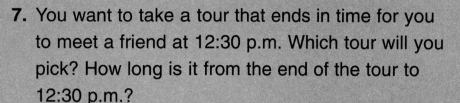

ON YOUR OWN

1. Why do you think some tours last longer than others? Why might two tours with the same name last different amounts of time?

2. The park opens at 7:00 a.m. and closes at 8:00 p.m. How many hours is this? How much time is there between the opening of the park and the first tour? Between the end of the last tour and closing time?

3. Talk to family members about a day at Timberlake Park. Invite each person to pick a tour that sounds interesting. Write a schedule for your family. When must you get to the park? When can you leave? How long will you be at the park altogether?

4. *My Journal:* What value does this activity have for you? Why?

EXPLORING
ELAPSED
TIME

HAND-y
REPRESENTATION

Have you ever wondered how people at different times or different places kept track of numbers?

In places around the world the hands and fingers were frequently used to represent data. In some languages the word for five and the word for hand were the same. Hands and fingers are a visual way of showing numbers and can be understood no matter what the language.

In American Indian picture writing, a hand drawn beside a tree could mean five trees.

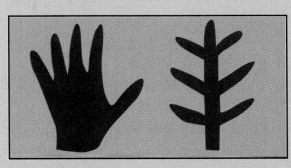

Buyers and sellers in Indian, Arabian and East African markets used a finger counting system for prices. Both buyers and sellers understood and, since no words were spoken, the deal was private.

1. Using American Indian notation, draw a picture which represents five boats.

2. If you count on your fingers, how do you represent six?

3. If you count on your fingers, how do you represent eleven?

4. Make up your own number system using your hands and fingers.

Time On Your Hands

Things to think about when you make a time line:

• How many hours are in a day?

• When does your time line begin? When does it end?

• Which hours are a.m.? Which are p.m.?

• Which activities will you include?

• How long will each activity last? In what order will the activities go?

• How will you show the times and the activities?

• What will you do if times don't come out even?

When you plan your ideal day, don't forget about—

• eating

• sleeping

• relaxing

You might make a chart like this to help you get started.

Activity for My Ideal Day	How Long It Lasts	Possible Start Time

old a Flake

▶ There are many ways you can make snowflakes.
Here is one way:

1. Fold your paper in half.

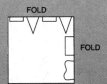

2. Then fold your paper in half again.

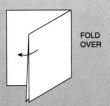

3. Cut holes along the folds. You can cut any shape holes you like.

4. Cut the edges any way you choose.

5. Open the paper and look at your snowflake.

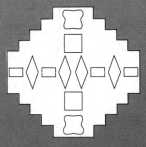

ON YOUR OWN

1. What shape will each hole be when you open up the paper?

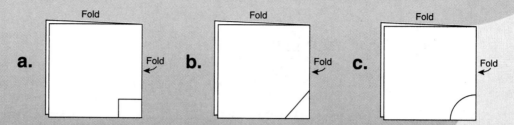

a. Fold / Fold

b. Fold / Fold

c. Fold / Fold

2. Find objects in your home that are box shapes, can shapes, ball shapes, and cone shapes. Make a bar graph to show how many of each shape you found.

3. *My Journal:* What do you now know about cutting paper to make snowflakes? Was this fun? Explain.

AMAZING
FACTS

No two snowflakes are said to be exactly the same. A snowflake can be made of as many as 100 snow crystals that cling together.

Gathering Data FOR A Pen Pal Class

Do you have a friend or relative who lives in another city? Maybe you can help set up the pen pal exchange! Talk with your teacher about what you could do.

Look for some sources for pen pal classes. Besides asking friends and relatives, how else could you find a pen pal class? Your class can write a letter that asks for information. Talk about the most important data you'd give in your very first letter.

Sarah Ramos
50 Summer Hill Road
Maynard, MA 01754

Pen Pal Class #3
Friendly School
2 Hope Drive
State of Mind, 12345

WORLDPOST
UNITED STATES POSTAL SERVICE
PAR AVION
AIR MAIL
LABEL 19-B, JUNE 1960

My Friends on the volley ball

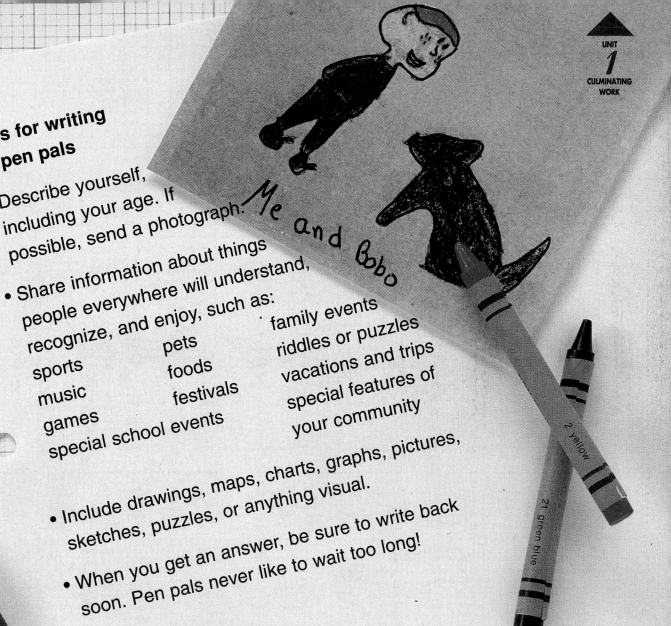

Tips for writing to pen pals

- Describe yourself, including your age. If possible, send a photograph.

- Share information about things people everywhere will understand, recognize, and enjoy, such as:

sports	pets	family events
music	foods	riddles or puzzles
games	festivals	vacations and trips
special school events		special features of your community

- Include drawings, maps, charts, graphs, pictures, sketches, puzzles, or anything visual.

- When you get an answer, be sure to write back soon. Pen pals never like to wait too long!

Check YOURSELF

Your data collection is complete and organized. You analyzed it and drew appropriate conclusions. You communicated these conclusions clearly in writing, and told how the data would help in a pen pal project.

Sports Stadium
Game Saturday
1:00 P.M.
Seat #105

Sports Stadium
Game Saturday
1:00 P.M.
Seat #103

How can we show numbers?

19

What's in a Name?

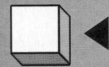

◀ 1 unit

◀ 1 ten or
10 units

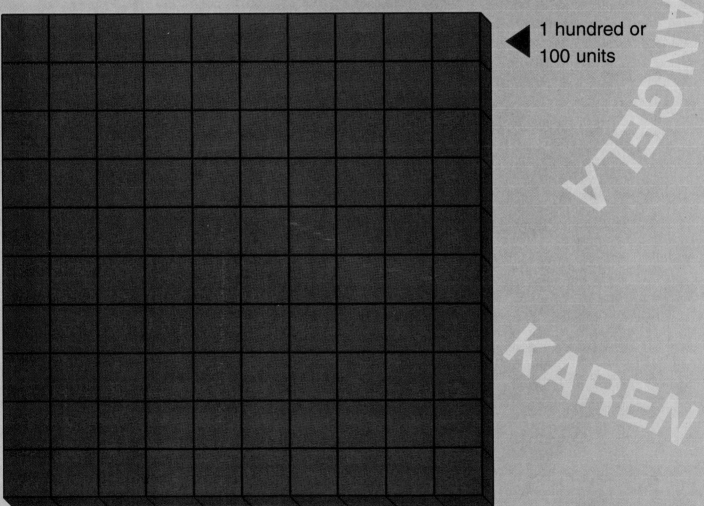

◀ 1 hundred or
100 units

► Write each number using symbols and words.

1.

2.

3.

4.

5.

6.

Draw blocks to show how many.

7. 496

8. two hundred thirty-four

9. 581

10. three hundred seventy-six

11. 405

12. five hundred sixty

13. *My Journal:* Write about the largest number you know. Where did you see it? What was it used for? Do you think it is an estimate or an exact number?

So Many Words!

About how many words are on the page all together?

Constitution

PREAMBLE

We, the people of the United States, in order to form a more perfect Union, establish justice, insure domestic tranquility, provide for the common defense, promote the general welfare, and secure the blessings of liberty to ourselves and our posterity do ordain and establish this Constitution for the United States of America.

ARTICLE 1.

Section 1—Legislative Powers; in whom vested:

All the legislative powers herein granted shall be vested in a Congress of the United States, which shall consist of a Senate and House of Representatives.

Section 2—House of Representatives, how and by whom chosen. Qualifications of a Representative. Representatives and direct taxes, how apportioned. Enumeration. Vacancies to be filled. Power of choosing officers, and of impeachment.

1. The House of Representatives shall be composed of members chosen every second year by the people of the several States, and the electors' in each State shall have the qualifications requisite for electors of the most numerous branch of the State Legislature.

ON YOUR OWN

1. Estimate how long it would take you to write your name 10,000 times. Then time yourself for one minute. Use this to find the approximate time it would take to write your name 10,000 times. Explain how you found your answer.

2. How high do you think 1,000 dinner plates would reach if they were stacked on top of one another? Tell how you decided.

3. Will you live to be 10,000 seconds old? 10,000 minutes? 10,000 days? About how many days might a typical person live? Explain your reasoning for each answer.

4. How high do you think 10,000 pennies would reach if they were stacked on top of one another? How far would they reach if they were placed side by side? Answer the same questions for dimes and quarters. Tell how you decided.

5. *My Journal:* Is it easier for you to estimate time or distance or length? Explain.

AMAZING FACTS

Every day, Americans process more than 33,000 bushels of peanuts into peanut butter. That's enough peanut butter to make a two-story house.

ESTIMATING
LARGER
NUMBERS

BUILD THE GREATER NUMBER
Game

Game Rules

1 Play with a partner. Arrange your place value cards in order in front of you.

2 Mix both players' sets of number cards together. Place them face down in the center.

3 Toss a number cube to see who goes first. The first player picks a number card and places it beneath one of the place value cards. Then the second player does the same.

4 Play until both you and your partner have chosen 4 number cards, and placed one number card beneath each place value card.

5 Say your numbers aloud. Compare numbers. Who built the greater number? That player is the winner.

THOUSANDS

HUNDREDS

Tip

You can also play a Build the Smaller Number Game with the same rules. In this game, the player with the smaller number is the winner.

ONES   TENS

Super Swamp Thing

Top Ten Scores

Ashley	84,398
Luwanda	69,254
Harold	73,190
Naomi	93,638
Ling Po	115,386
Cesar	63,589
Maria	83,127
David	90,475
Colin	85,378
Lamont	93,587

ON YOUR OWN

1. Tell which is the greater number.
   27,804 or 25,976   9,785 or 11,312
   Write and tell how you decided
   which of the two numbers
   is greater.

2. Carmen says that she just
   "lines up" the numbers to tell
   which is greater. What do you think she means?
   Show an example to explain her method. Would
   this method work for comparing three numbers?
   Four numbers? Why or why not?

3. Look for patterns to find the missing numbers.

   a. 750, 1000, 1250, 1500, 1750, ⬚, ⬚, ⬚
   b. 1200, 2400, 3600, ⬚, 6000, 7200, ⬚, ⬚
   c. 1332, 2432, 3532, 4632, ⬚, ⬚, ⬚, ⬚

4. Make up a pattern problem like one of the ones
   in problem 3. Exchange with a classmate to
   solve. Check each other's work.

5. What category on the left accounts
   for the most recycled material? How
   did you determine your answer?

6. Is more glass or newspaper recycled?
   Tell how you decided.

7. How much did the Recycling Center
   earn for its efforts? How did you decide?

8. Write and tell how you would order all
   the amounts of materials that were
   recycled from least to greatest.

9. *My Journal:* What was most interesting
   about the video activity you did?

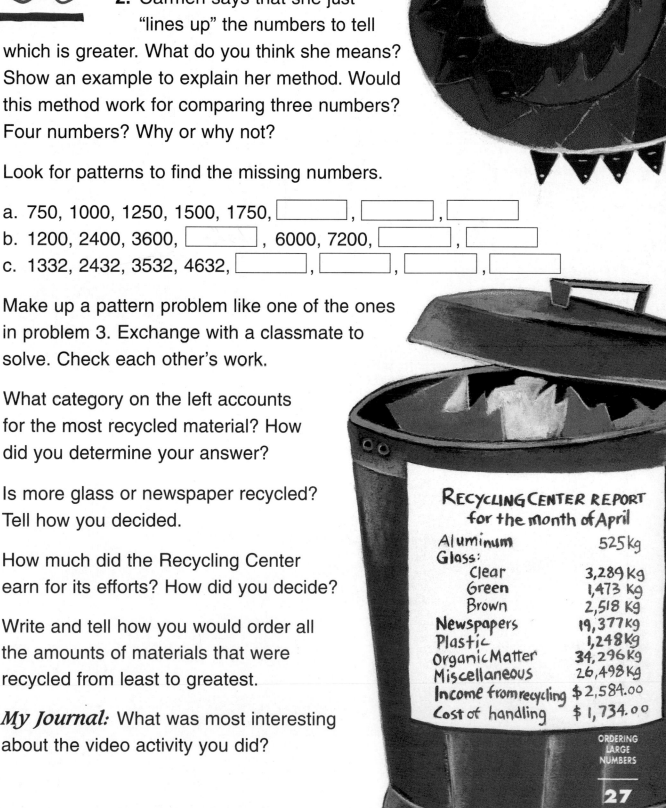

RECYCLING CENTER REPORT
for the month of April

Aluminum	525 kg
Glass:	
Clear	3,289 kg
Green	1,473 kg
Brown	2,518 kg
Newspapers	19,377 kg
Plastic	1,248 kg
Organic Matter	34,296 kg
Miscellaneous	26,498 kg
Income from recycling	$2,584.00
Cost of handling	$1,734.00

ORDERING
LARGE
NUMBERS

Counting with WOLVES

Have you ever wondered how people in different times or places represented large numbers? A bone from a young wolf that died thirty thousand years ago was found in Czechoslovakia. The bone has 55 notches arranged in two groups, 25 in the first group and 30 in the second. Do you think what this represents? Is it 55? Within each group the notches are arranged in groups of five.

Africans from the area that is now Zaire used marks on a bone to record numbers also.

The Ishango bone is an example. Researchers are not sure whether the marks show a number system or a type of calendar. What do you think?

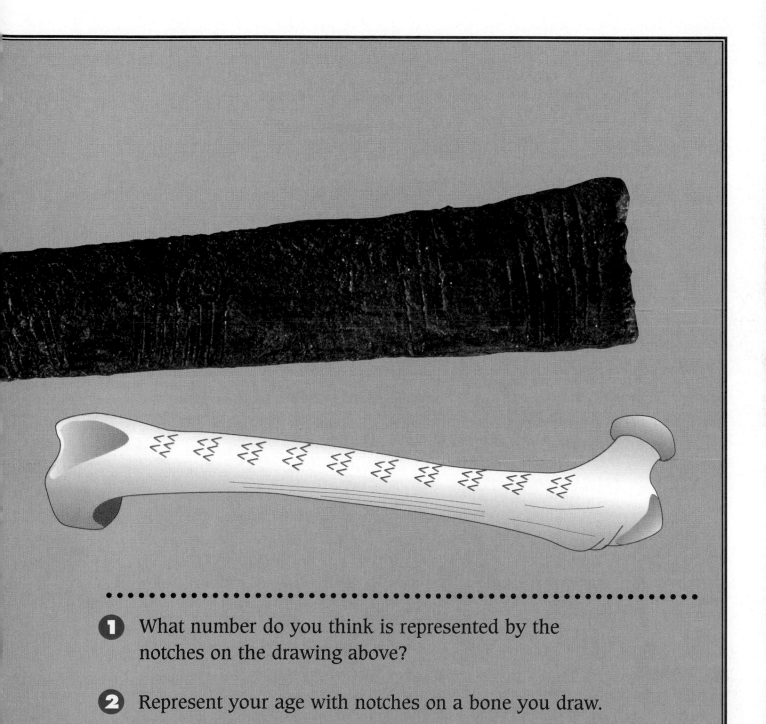

1 What number do you think is represented by the notches on the drawing above?

2 Represent your age with notches on a bone you draw.

3 Represent the total number in your class with "bone" notation.

STRAIGHTSHOOTER

Game Rules
. . . .

Put the 12 scores from
page 31 on your spinner.

You get 5 shots or spins.
A total of 35,000 points or
more wins a free game.

Different shots can land on
the same number.
Good Luck!!

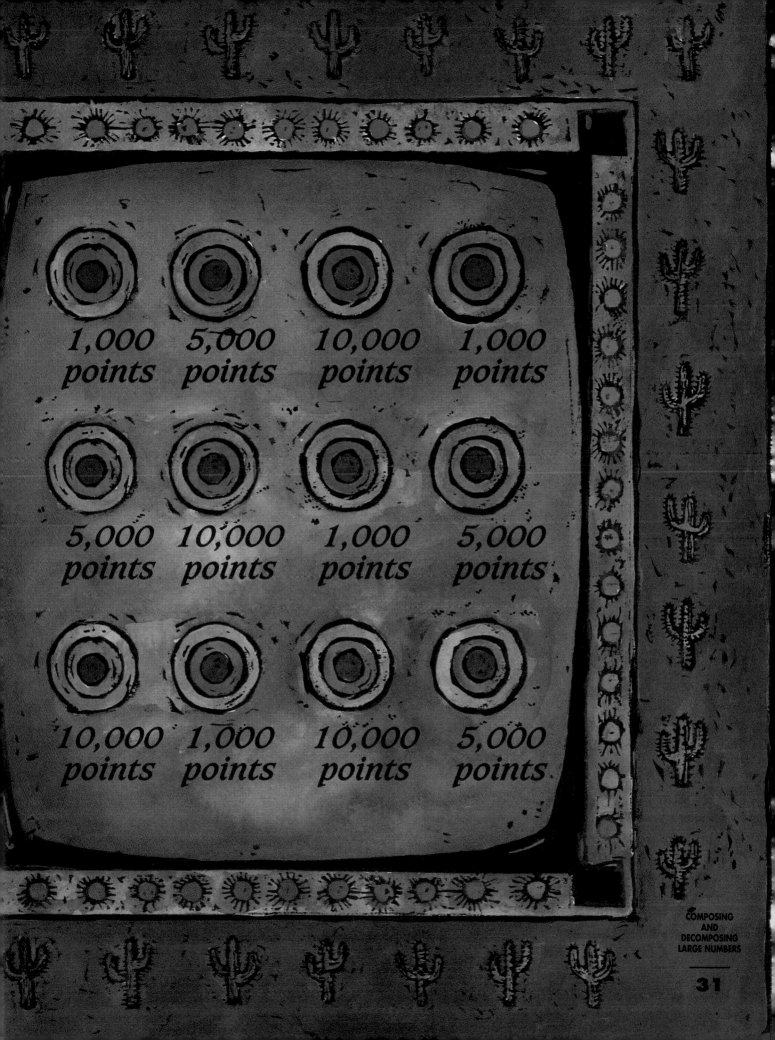

1,000
points

5,000
points

10,000
points

1,000
points

5,000
points

10,000
points

1,000
points

5,000
points

10,000
points

1,000
points

10,000
points

5,000
points

ON YOUR OWN

1. How many ways can you get a score of 12,000 in Straightshooter? A score of 25,000? A score of 44,000?

2. Make up a video game and a set of rules that would allow you to win a free game more than half the time.

   a. Explain why you might win so often.

   b. What would be the greatest possible score on your game?

   c. What would be the least possible score, if you had no misses? How did you decide?

300 pts

2,000 pts

750 pts

1,000 pts

250 pts

100 pts

3. How does the possible score of your game compare with scores of other video games you have played or seen?

4. *My Journal:* What questions do you have about games like these?

Be a Winner!

Congratulations

$100,000.00

1. Suppose you chose to get the Grand Prize in equal payments over 10 years. How much would you get each year? Write and show how you decided what you get paid each year.

2. Suppose you chose to get the Grand Prize in equal payments over 20 years. How much would you get each year? Write and show how you decided.

MORE
COMPOSING AND
DECOMPOSING

Showing Large Numbers

What does
10,000 look like?

Lots of leaves?

Many ants?

Plenty of candy?

Use centimeter grid paper to find a way to show the number 10,000. Write and tell how you are sure your model shows 10,000. Be sure to make your model easy for someone else to understand.

5,406

5,407

5,408

5,409

7,849

7,851

7,850

7,852

Check **Y**OURSELF

Your model for 10,000 was clear and easy to understand. You explained clearly in writing why the model shows 10,000 and told how groupings of ten were used in your model.

What are addition and subtraction?

Legs in the Barnyard

Don't look now, but there are 13 chickens and pigs playing in the barnyard. Altogether there are a total of 36 legs. How many chickens and how many pigs are playing in the barnyard?

ON YOUR OWN

▶ Solve the problems below about Legs, Heads, Wheels, Tables, and Chairs. Explain your solution.

1. Farmer Fred has a total of 12 ducks and sheep. Altogether, these animals have 38 legs. How many ducks and how many sheep does Fred have?

2. The Country Kitchen restaurant has 13 4-legged tables and 3-legged stools altogether. If there are a total of 42 table and stool legs in the restaurant, how many tables and how many stools are there?

3. In the park, Dwayne was under the picnic table playing with a grasshopper. From there he saw 15 bicycles and tricycles pass by. If he counted a total of 36 wheels, how many bicycles were there? How many tricycles?

4. Rashida has pets. Altogether, they have 12 legs and 4 heads. What pets could Rashida have and how many of each does she have?

5. *My Journal:* Which problem was most interesting to you? Explain.

AMAZING
F A C T S

The world's largest table was set up in Spain in 1986. It was nearly a mile long and was used to seat 6,400 people!

Side by Side

▶ Solve. Use reasoning and Power Polygons.

1. You have some triangles and squares. There are more squares than triangles. There are 18 sides altogether. How many triangles and how many squares do you have?

2. You have the same number of triangles and squares. There are 35 sides altogether. How many triangles and how many squares do you have?

3. You have squares and hexagons with a total of 22 sides. How many squares do you have? How many hexagons?

4. You have squares and triangles. Altogether, there are 20 sides. How many squares and how many triangles do you have?

5. You have triangles and hexagons with a total of 24 sides. How many triangles and how many hexagons do you have?

6. You have triangles, squares, and hexagons. There are the same number of hexagons as triangles. There are 30 sides altogether. How many squares, triangles, and hexagons do you have?

ON YOUR OWN

▶ Solve. Use reasoning and Power Polygons.
Draw pictures of the shapes if it helps.

1. You have some squares and triangles. There
are fewer squares. Altogether, there are 34
sides. How many squares and how many
triangles do you have?

2. You have only triangles and hexagons.
Altogether, there are 15 sides. How many
triangles and hexagons do you have?

3. You have hexagons and squares with a total
of 36 sides. How many of each shape do you
have? How would this problem change if you
used rectangles instead of squares?

4. Make up two shape problems of
your own. Try to write one that
has more than one solution.
Record your answers.

5. *My Journal:* Which problems
that you solved were easy?
Difficult? Explain why.

Home on the Range

▶ Try these estimations. Check each estimate you make with a calculator. If your sum does not fall within the range, try again with another number.

What number do I add to 277
to get a sum between 600 and 700?

1. 32 + _____ ; range: 80-90

2. 87 + _____ ; range: 120-130

3. 274 + _____ ; range: 600-700

4. 316 + _____ ; range: 800-900

5. 438 + _____ ; range: 730-780

6. 73 + _____ ; range: 520-560

7. 198 + _____ ; range: 900-975

8. 582 + _____ ; range: 750-770

ON YOUR OWN

▶ Estimate the number of boxes, cartons, and cases needed for the horseshoes. Then find the exact number for each. Use your calculator. Compare your estimate with your exact answer.

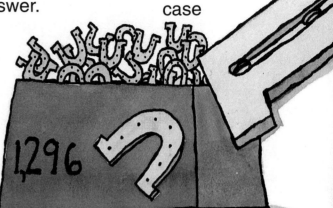

case

carton

box

36

216

1,296

1. Horseshoes = 144

_____ boxes

_____ cartons

_____ cases

2. Horseshoes = 648

_____ boxes

_____ cartons

_____ cases

3. Horseshoes = 1,512

_____ boxes

_____ cartons

_____ cases

4. Horseshoes = 2,016

_____ boxes

_____ cartons

_____ cases

5. Horseshoes = 1,728

_____ boxes

_____ cartons

_____ cases

6. *My Journal:* What did you find out about ranges?

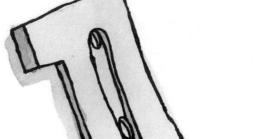

Problems, Problems, Problems

▶ Estimate each sum. Then find the exact answer.

Chalkboard Talk

1. $37 + 19 = $ _____
2. What is $48 + 43$? _____
3. What is the sum of 59 and 63? _____
4. $126 + 319 = $ _____
5. Find 606 and 244 _____
6. What is the sum of 372 and 77? _____

7. $\begin{array}{r} 156 \\ + 737 \\ \hline \end{array}$

8. $\begin{array}{r} 438 \\ + 551 \\ \hline \end{array}$

ON YOUR OWN

▶ Build the pizza you think your family would enjoy. Decide what size it will be. Choose your favorite toppings. Find the total cost.

Pizzas

Huge $15.50
Large $12.75
Medium $10.00
Small $8.25
Tiny $6.95

Toppings

35¢ each

Xtra Cheese
Chocolate Chips
Onions
Mushrooms
Peppers
Popcorn

My Journal:
Write and explain
if this problem
was easy or difficult
for you and why.

CLOSING IN ON 1,000

Group

This is a game for two players.

Materials

Each pair needs 4 sets of 0-9 number cards.

Game Rules

1 Shuffle all the cards. Place them face down in a stack.

2 In turn, each player draws 1, 2, or 3 cards from the deck and records the number formed by the cards in the order they were drawn. For example, if you draw a 5, then a 7, and then a 3, your number is 573.

3 Each player returns the cards to the stack and shuffles. Then each player takes another turn. This time the player can draw zero, 1, 2, or 3 cards and adds the new number formed to the first number.

4 Players continue taking turns, adding each new number formed to the total.

5 The game continues until one player gets a sum over 1,000. The player with the sum closer to 1,000 wins.

6 If there is a tie, each player draws a card, and the player with the greater number wins.

ON YOUR OWN

▶ Imagine that you are playing a game of Closing in on 1,000 with a partner named Ed. You have each drawn three times. So far, these are the sums each of you has made:

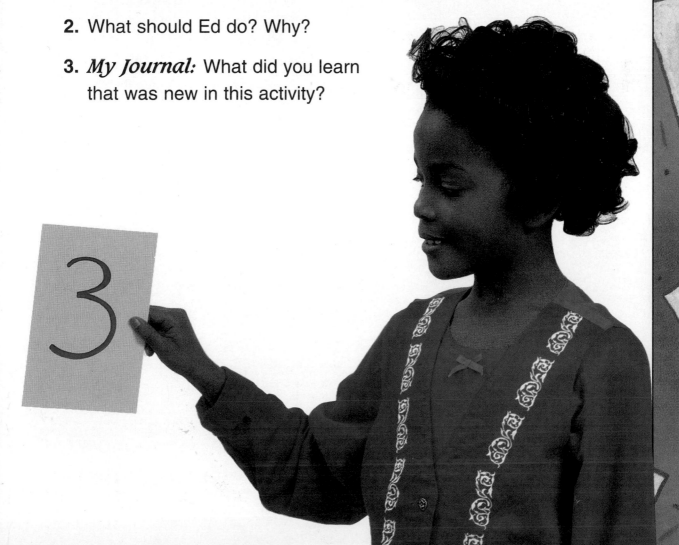

My draws
```
   273
 + 465
   738
 + 156
   894
```

Ed's draws
```
   089
 + 327
   416
 + 543
   959
```

Look at the two running totals.

1. Will you draw any cards? If so, how many? Explain.

2. What should Ed do? Why?

3. *My Journal:* What did you learn that was new in this activity?

The CASE OF THE Missing ARROW

Have you ever wondered how people in different times or different places counted and compared? This American Indian tale tells about one common way.

Little Eagle was 9 years old and his task was to guard a stack of arrows. He did not know the names of numbers, but he always knew if even one arrow were missing. He gathered rocks—one for each arrow—and placed them in a pile next to the arrows.

One day he saw that there were fewer arrows than rocks, so he knew some arrows were missing. He looked all over until he saw his little sister playing with the arrows. When he put the missing arrows back, he saw there were as many arrows as rocks.

Across the ocean a similar system was in use. Because some African people believed that it was bad luck to count animals, a herder would put one small stone in a bag for each animal and then match them to the animals one-to-one.

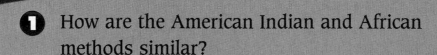

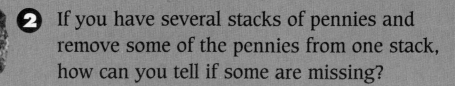

❶ How are the American Indian and African methods similar?

❷ If you have several stacks of pennies and remove some of the pennies from one stack, how can you tell if some are missing?

Big Hand

▶ You can do an experiment to find out who has the biggest hand. Here's how:

1. Get a jar large enough to put your hand in.

2. Use a centimeter ruler to mark and label a strip of paper from 0 to 25 centimeters in half centimeters. Tape this strip onto the side of the jar.

3. Fill the jar with enough water to cover anyone's hand completely. Measure its water level to the nearest half centimeter. Record this measurement in a table.

4. Place your hand into the jar. Find the water level now. Record it in the table, too.

5. Find the difference between water levels. Record this in your table. What have you learned about hand sizes in your group?

Take it Away!

▶ Estimate each difference. Then find the exact answer.

Chalkboard Talk

1. $42 - 16 = $ _____

2. What is $56 - 33$? _____

3. What is the difference between 73 and 37? _____

4. $329 - 114 = $ _____

5. Find $656 - 244$ _____

6. What is the difference between 382 and 66? _____

7. $\begin{array}{r} 717 \\ -534 \\ \hline \end{array}$

8. $\begin{array}{r} 852 \\ -351 \\ \hline \end{array}$

A frog is at the bottom of a well that is 50 meters deep. It is trying to get out.

Each day the frog climbs up 8 meters. But at night, it slides back down 3 meters.

1. How many days will it take the frog to climb out of the well? Show all your work. Be prepared to explain how you found your answer.

2. *My Journal:* Did you think this was a difficult problem? Write and solve your own problem that is something like this one.

When is an Estimate Enough?

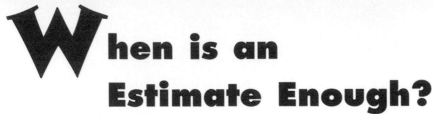

▶ Pretend that your class is planning a bean bag toss game for a school fun fair. The game is similar to the one below. There are a few questions you need to answer in planning your game. Tell whether you need to calculate or measure or whether an estimate will do.

1. How big will the game board be? What will its dimensions be?

2. What materials will you need to make the game? How much will they cost?

3. How many points will be for each hole and how many points are needed to win?

ON YOUR OWN

▶ The school principal, Ms. Worrier, needs to find out the answers to some questions before she will allow a fun fair to be held in the gym.

Read the questions she has. Decide whether each will need an exact answer or if an estimate will do. Explain your choice.

1. How many people will be in the gym at one time?

2. For how many hours will the gym be needed?

3. How many game booths will be there? How much room will each booth need?

4. How much time will classes need to prepare their games?

5. How much will tickets sell for? How many will be printed?

6. If I send letters home to parents, how much money should I recommend children bring with them to the fair?

7. How much money will we raise for the school at this fair?

8. *My Journal:* Which question was the most difficult to answer? Why?

DECIDING
WHEN TO
ESTIMATE

Munchy Meals at Mike's

The Main Stuff

Chicken taco	$.89
Corn dog	$.75
Veggie burger	$1.19
Giant salad	$1.25
Buffalo burger	$1.39
Stomper	$.89
Double Stomper	$1.49

The Side Stuff

Cole slaw	$.65
Curly fries	$.75
Plantains	$.45
Tomato salad	$.59

The Wet Stuff

Soda	$.59
Lemonade	$.69
Iced tea	$.39

The Sweet Stuff

Fruit cup	$.59
Pudding	$.49
Chocolate cake	$.95
Giant cookie	$.35

▶ Show the menu at Mike's to two members of your family. Do this before dinner, so they'll be hungry.

Ask each of them to use the menu to plan his or her favorite meal. (If they don't like this menu, let them choose a menu they do like!)

Whichever menu they choose, tell your family members to write down their choices and present them to you.

1. Estimate and then find the total cost of each meal. Write down these amounts.

2. Create a Munchy Meal for each person. Figure out the savings. Ask each person to check your work.

3. *My Journal:* What did you learn from this activity?

Foods

Can of dog or
cat food: $.79
Dry food for dogs
or cats: $8 – $30
for a 20-pound bag

Pet Care Costs

How much does it cost to keep a dog or a cat for
one year?

At an animal shelter, it can cost about $55 to buy
a dog. A cat costs about $45.

The costs of some things your pet will need are
given. Think about how long some of these
supplies will last.

Medical Care

Rx

Visit to vet: $60
Rabies or distemper shots:
$12 each
Leukemia shots: 3 for $4 each
Spaying or neutering: $75
Flea or tick powder:
$7.59

Toys, Equipment, and other thin...

Dog license $4.50

Dog or cat collar:
$4.95–$19.95

Leash: $6.95–$22.95

Kitty litter: 8 pound
for $3.95

Brush: $3.00

rubber chew toys:
$2–$6.95

$\mathscr{C}$heck**YOURSELF**

Your plan is complete in all ways. It shows that
you understand how to use addition and subtraction.
You added and subtracted successfully to find all
costs. Your estimates of expenses are reasonable.
Your written plan communicated your ideas
clearly to others.

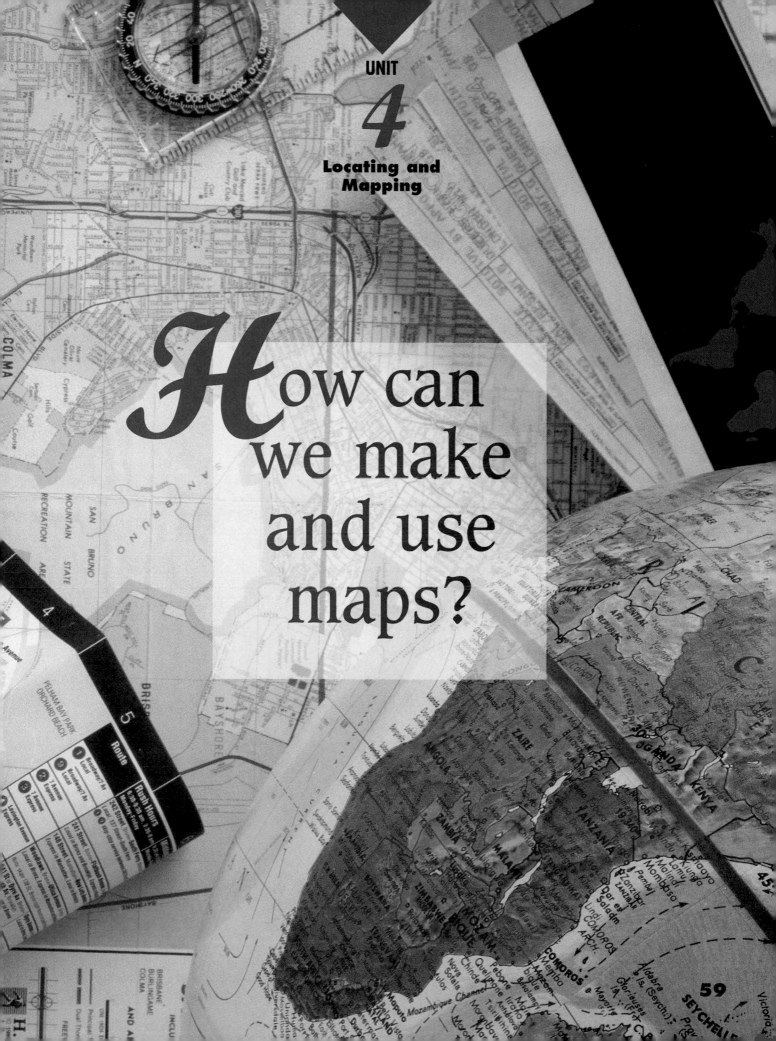

*H*ow can
we make
and use
maps?

Know Your Place!

 ap That Picture

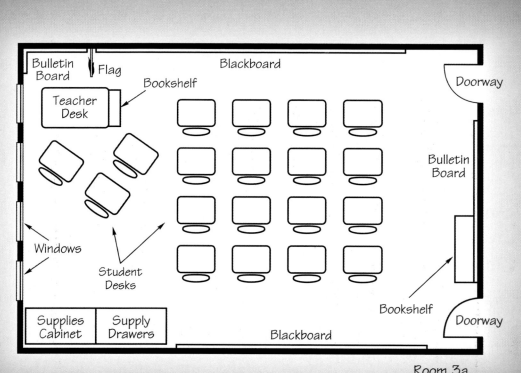

Room 3a
Classroom

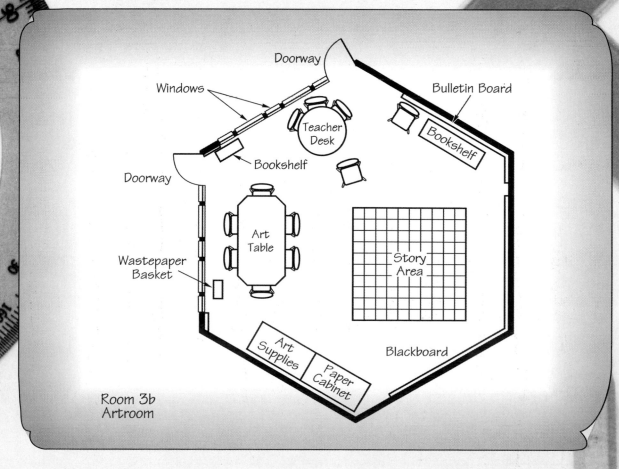

Room 3b
Artroom

SEA SHELL MAPS

Have you ever wondered if there were different ways to make maps?

Maps were frequently made from handy materials. Some of the earliest maps were made by the Babylonians on tablets of damp clay that were baked in the sun. Chinese people used their beautiful silk fabrics for map making.

Some of the most interesting maps were made by Polynesian Islanders in the South Pacific. They made maps from reeds, sea shells, and palm leaves. The reeds made a grid, the shells represented islands, and the curved leaves represented the ocean's waves and currents.

1 Using some handy materials, make a map of your neighborhood.

2 Pretend you are burying treasure somewhere nearby. Draw a map to show where it is buried.

3 When someone sends you a birthday card, how does the postal worker find your home to deliver it?

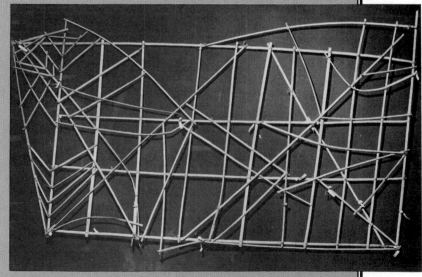

Reed Map

Getting From Here to There

1. Write directions for going from your home to school.

2. Write directions for going from school to your home. How do they differ from the directions in problem 1?

3. What directions would you give to help fire fighters, police, or an ambulance get to your home in an emergency?

4. Mazes appear in many places. A maze like this one appears on a Navajo blanket. Explain how you would get from the X to the Y, staying within the spaces and not crossing any lines.

5. *My Journal:* What did you learn about directions from this activity? Explain.

Where Is It?

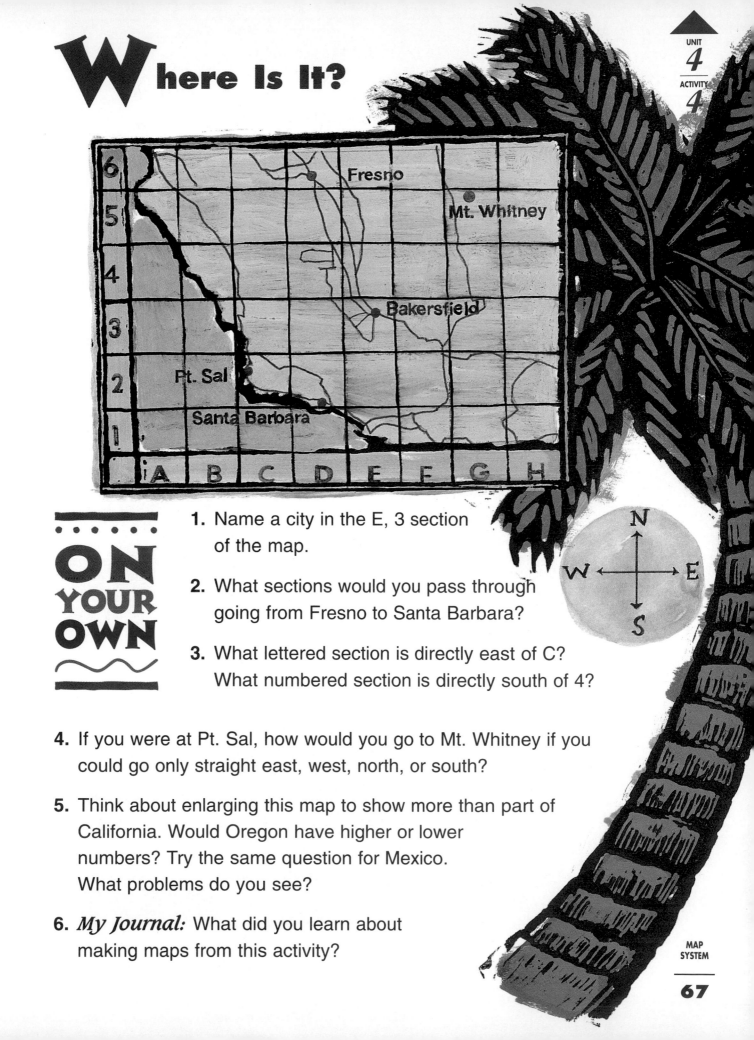

ON YOUR OWN

1. Name a city in the E, 3 section of the map.

2. What sections would you pass through going from Fresno to Santa Barbara?

3. What lettered section is directly east of C? What numbered section is directly south of 4?

4. If you were at Pt. Sal, how would you go to Mt. Whitney if you could go only straight east, west, north, or south?

5. Think about enlarging this map to show more than part of California. Would Oregon have higher or lower numbers? Try the same question for Mexico. What problems do you see?

6. *My Journal:* What did you learn about making maps from this activity?

DINOSAUR DISCOVERY

Materials

5 sets of markers to represent the 5 dinosaurs (for each player)

Copy of map grid

Rules

1 Use the game grid. Place your sets of small markers that stand for dinosaurs on any row or column of squares on the grid.

2 Take turns with your partner guessing the location of each other's dinosaur markers. Use letter-number pairs.

3 The first one to find all of their partner's dinosaur markers wins!

Diplodocus

Tyrannosaurus Rex

Stegosaurus

MAKING MAPS

Have you ever made a map? What was the map for? What are some things that should be on a good map?

Work with your group to make a map of your school so that family and friends can find their way around. Some things to think about:

- What things should go on the map? What doesn't need to be on the map?

- How can pairs of numbers or letters help someone use your map?

- Where would be the best places in the school to have the map?

Animals are most active in the early morning and late afternoon. We suggest catching our animal shows mid-day while our other creatures are napping.

Restrooms

Telephone

CheckYOURSELF

The map you made is complete and easy to use. It includes all the important places in your school. You explained clearly in writing how pairs of numbers or letters were used in your map.

How can we use equal groups?

Twice as Nice

For about every 89 births there is one set of twins born. Identical twins occur once in about 1,000 births.

The constellation Gemini is called the twin constellation. Can you see why?

AMAZING
FACTS

Triplets occur about once in 7,900 births.

Quadruplets occur about once in 705,000 births.

Every year there is a national festival of twins. Twins come from all over the country—and world. Prizes are awarded for twins who look most alike and least alike.

Up to 100!

1	2	3	4	5	6	7	8	9	10
11	12	13	14	15	16	17	18	19	20
21	22	23	24	25	26	27	28	29	30
31	32	33	34	35	36	37	38	39	40
41	42	43	44	45	46	47	48	49	50
51	52	53	54	55	56	57	58	59	60
61	62	63	64	65	66	67	68	69	70
71	72	73	74	75	76	77	78	79	80
81	82	83	84	85	86	87	88	89	90
91	92	93	94	95	96	97	98	99	100

ON YOUR OWN

1. Use the Hundred Chart to record the numbers you land on when you count by 3. Use the same Hundred Chart to record the numbers you land on when you count by 6. Write about patterns you see.

2. Try shading in a Hundred Chart with another pair of numbers between 2 and 10. Write about what you observe. Compare with problem 1.

3. Write and predict what will happen if you try another pair of numbers between 2 and 10. Use another Hundred Chart and count by the two numbers you selected. Write about what actually happened.

4. Write about patterns you can find when counting by groups of equal numbers on a Hundred Chart. Include an example of a pattern you discovered.

5. *My Journal:* Which problem was the most difficult? Explain. Which was the most interesting? Explain.

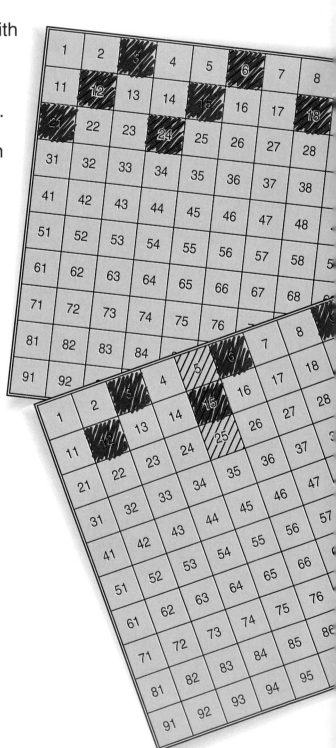

The Cost of Stamps

How many stamps are on a page?

How many pages are in a book?

How many stamps are there in all?

What is the total cost for all of the stamps?

How could you find the total cost if the stamps cost 23¢ each?

ON YOUR OWN

1. How many stamps are in each book? What does each book of stamps cost?

a.

b. 3 rows of 4 stamps each, 3 sheets in the book
Each stamp costs 15¢.

2. Ramona has $10. Can she buy 2 books of Olympic stamps?

3. You can buy stamped envelopes from the United States Postal Service. These stamped envelopes cost 34¢ each (29¢ for the stamp, 5¢ for the envelope). Write a multiplication equation for the cost of 10 of these envelopes.

For a stronger America, count us in!
43 million people with disabilities
USA 29

Trish Gorman
1526 Oak St. Apt. 3
PEEKSKILL, N.Y. 10566

4. Draw an arrangement of 20 stamps. Write a multiplication equation for your arrangement.

5. Give your stamps a value. Write a multiplication equation to tell what your stamps are worth.

Stamps often come in coils or rolls of 100, 500, and 3,000. Write a multiplication equation for each of these.

6. Coil of 100

USA 23
Mary Cassatt

7. Coil of 500

RR Caboose 1890s
USA 11c
Bulk Rate

8. *My Journal:* What did you learn that was new?

Quilt Patterns

What patterns do you see
in the quilts?

X	0	1	2	3	4	5
0						
1		▪	▪▪	▪▪▪	▪▪▪▪	▪▪▪▪▪
2		▪	▪▪			▪▪▪
3		▪	▪▪	3 x 4 = 12		
4		▪	▪▪	▪▪▪		▪▪▪▪

ON YOUR OWN

G	r	e	g
G	r	e	g
G	r	e	g
G	r	e	g
G	r	e	g
G	r	e	g
G	r	e	g

1. Make a word quilt pattern that is an array. Use your first name and as many rows as you like.

2. Write a multiplication equation that tells the number of letters in your first name quilt.

3. Make a quilt pattern for your last name. Write a multiplication fact for your pattern.

4. How does the drawing for 3 x 4 look like the drawing for 4 x 3? How are they different? What about 1 x 5 and 5 x 1?

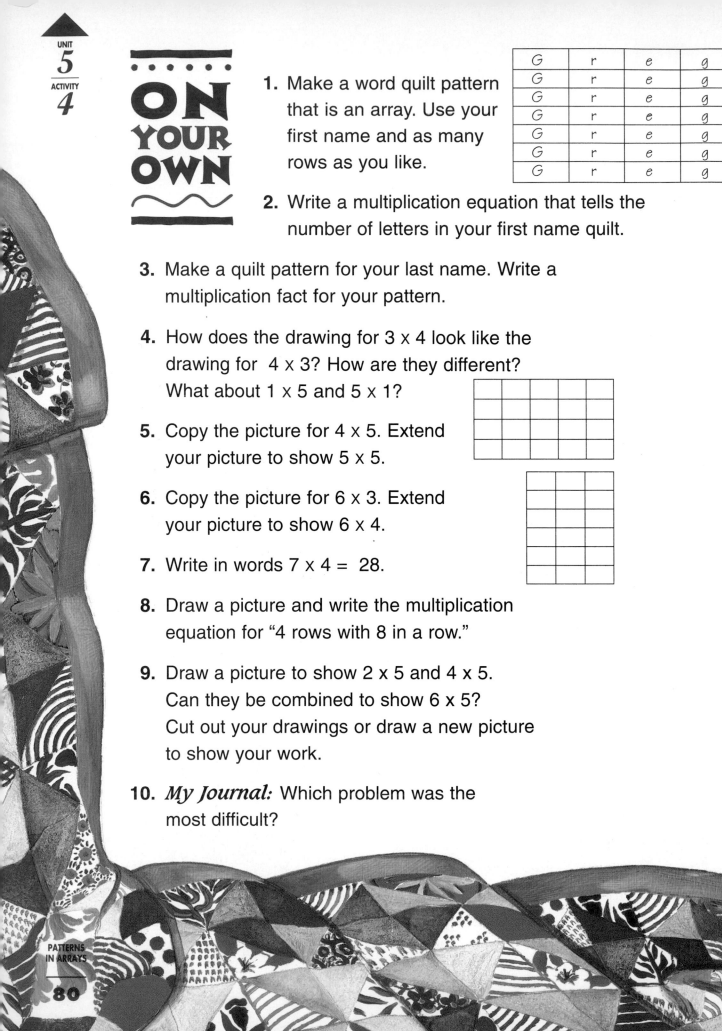

5. Copy the picture for 4 x 5. Extend your picture to show 5 x 5.

6. Copy the picture for 6 x 3. Extend your picture to show 6 x 4.

7. Write in words 7 x 4 = 28.

8. Draw a picture and write the multiplication equation for "4 rows with 8 in a row."

9. Draw a picture to show 2 x 5 and 4 x 5. Can they be combined to show 6 x 5? Cut out your drawings or draw a new picture to show your work.

10. *My Journal:* Which problem was the most difficult?

ARE YOU GAME?

Have you ever wondered about the kinds of games people played before there were video games?

American Indians, known as Haida, who live in the Pacific Northwest, played a stick game that made use of both their reasoning and wood carving skills. The Haida played the game with 18 beautifully carved sticks with different designs.

You and a partner can play a version of the game by using 18 counters. Mark one of the counters on the bottom with a piece of tape. You divide the counters into equal groups and your partner gets a certain number of chances to guess which group the marked counter is in.

1 How many different equal groups can you divide the counters into?

2 Why do you think 18 was chosen as the number of sticks? What other number might be a good choice? What number would be a bad choice?

3 If you divide your counters into 6 groups should your partner have more or fewer chances to guess than if you divide the counters into 2 groups?

THE ARRAY game

Group

3 players, 1 banker

Materials

Each group needs:
Eight sets of array cards for each of these:
1-by-1, 1-by-2, 1-by-3, 1-by-4, 1-by-5,
2-by-2, 2-by-3, 2-by-4, 2-by-5, 3-by-3,
3-by-4, 3-by-5, 4-by-4, 4-by-5 and 5-by-5.
A pair of number cubes
showing 1,2,3,4,5, and W

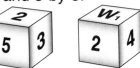

Each player needs:
A 100-square gameboard or
grid paper

1	2	3	4	5	6	7	8	9	10
11	12	13	14	15	16	17	18	19	20
21	22	23	24	25	26	27	28	29	30
31	32	33	34	35	36	37	38	39	40
41	42	43	44	45	46	47	48	49	50
51	52	53	54	55	56	57	58	59	60
61	62	63	64	65	66	67	68	69	70
71	72	73	74	75	76	77	78	79	80
81	82	83	84	85	86	87	88	89	90
91	92	93	94	95	96	97	98	99	100

Game Rules

1 The banker keeps all the array cards.

2 The player to the right of the banker
rolls the number cubes and names the
product of the 2 numbers that are face
up on the cubes. Note: If "W" comes
up, choose a "Wild Number" – any
number from 1 to 5.

3 The banker gives the player an array
card for the product.

4 The player places the array card
anywhere on his/her gameboard.
Once the array card is placed, it
CANNOT be moved.

5 The other two players take turns.
The game continues until one player
completely fills her or his gameboard
and WINS!

6 Play again with a different banker.

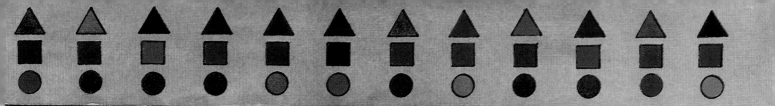

Sometimes the array for a set of rolled numbers will not fit on the gameboard. You break apart the product and ask for smaller array cards.

Example

Two 5s were rolled.
So 25 is the product.

The 5-by-5 array card looks like this: It doesn't fit in the space left on the board.

5 X 5 = 25

But a 1-by-5 and a 4-by-5 might fit.

Or a 2-by-5 and a 3-by-5 might fit.

1 X 5 = 5
4 X 5 = 20
5 X 5 = 25

If none of the pairs of smaller arrays works, the next player takes a turn.

Would any of the smaller arrays fit on this part of the gameboard?

2 X 5 = 10
3 X 5 = 15
5 X 5 = 25

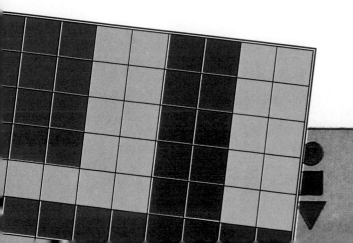

Collecting Coins

Korean Won

Coin albums usually have equal rows.

How many rows?

How many in each row?

How many coins altogether?

42 Italian Lire

Solve. Use any method you like. Tell how you solved the problem.

How many in each row?

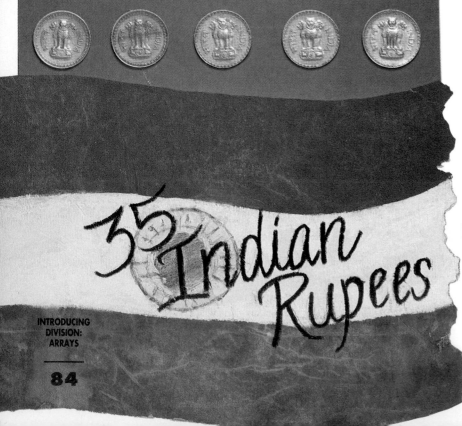

35 Indian Rupees

How many rows are needed?

▶ Solve. Use any method you like.
Tell how you solved the problem.

Carrie was given 50 collector coins and
a new coin album for her birthday.

There are 6 rows on a page, and one
row in the coin album holds 5 coins.

How many pages does Carrie
need for her coins? How many
rows does she need?

Fair Shares

How many each?

How many each?

How many each?

35 party favors
How many for each bag?

8 monsters on a sheet
How many sheets
are needed?

▶ Solve. Use any method you like.
Tell how you solved the problem.

7 sheets of stickers
How many on each sheet?

Six girls bought a
booklet of stickers to share.
They want to share them
equally. How many stickers
should each one get?

Showing Division

Solve these problems.
Show your work and record your answer.

3 stacks of comic books

27 comic books

How many comic books in each stack?

9 rows
How many rocks in each row?

How many battery packs in the box?

ON YOUR OWN

▶ Solve these problems. Record your work using division symbols.

1. 25 videos
How many showcases are needed?

5 Videos

2. 38 postcards

7 album pages

How many cards on each?

Here is some data about children's collections. Copy and complete the chart. Write the problem and answer with division symbols.

Student	Number of rows	Number in each row	Remainder	Number in all
3. Ivan's ivy plants	3			18
4. Marge's magnets		7		28
5. Elias's eggs	5		2	32
6. Jorge's hats		9		45
7. Melba's miniature mice		4	1	17

8. *My Journal:* Which problem was the most difficult? Why?

EXTENDING
DIVISION
UNDERSTANDING

What's the Question?

▶ Write a question for each situation. Then solve the problem any way you choose.

15 days
7 days in a week

23 potholders
8 campers

▶ Use the pictures. Write a problem and solve it.

5 tents
8 campers
in each

Bag of 56 marshmallows
6 sticks

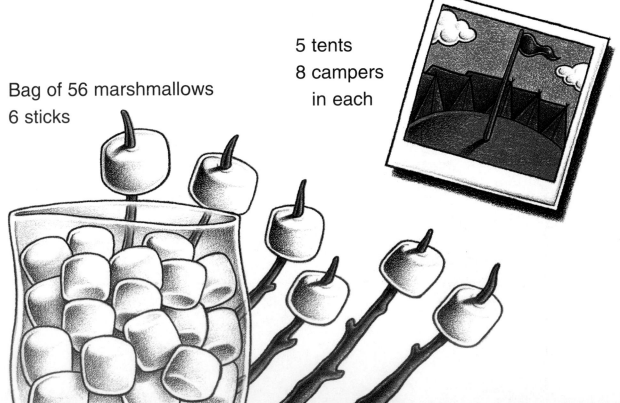

ON YOUR OWN

▶ Write a question. Then solve your problem any way you choose.

1. 45 campers
   8 fit in each van

2. 9 players on a team
   5 teams

3. 34 floating buoys
   8 lines

THE TIGERS

4.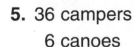

5. 36 campers
   6 canoes

6.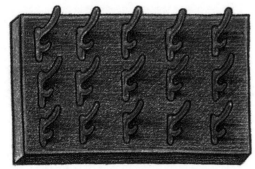

7. Write your own division problem. Write a division equation for it and tell how you solved the problem.

8. Draw a picture of a multiplication or division situation. Write a question and answer it.

9. *My Journal:* Is there anything about division you do not understand? Explain your difficulties.

Land On "0" Game

Group
Pairs

Materials

Each pair needs:
2 different-colored markers

2 Hundred Charts
(with 0 written in)

2 number cubes
one numbered 1 to 6
one numbered 0, 7, 8,
9, W_1, W_2

2 score sheets

calculator

Game Rules

❶ Each person writes 0
on her or his Hundred Chart
and rolls the 2 cubes. The
person who can make the
larger 2-digit number
is the first player.
(W₁ can be any
number from 0 to 4;
W₂ can be any
number from 5 to 9.)

❷ The first player puts a
marker on any number of
his or her choice on the
Hundred Chart and then
rolls the number cube
numbered from 1 to 6.

❸ The player then tries to jump
backward to 0 from the marker by
the number rolled, keeping track of
the number of jumps and seeing
if 0 will be landed on or if
there is a remainder.

Marked Number	Number Rolled	Jumps	Remainder
27	5	5	2

❹ The player writes the
division statement and
records only the remainder
on the score sheet.

Score
2

1	2
11	1
21	
31	
41	
51	
	6

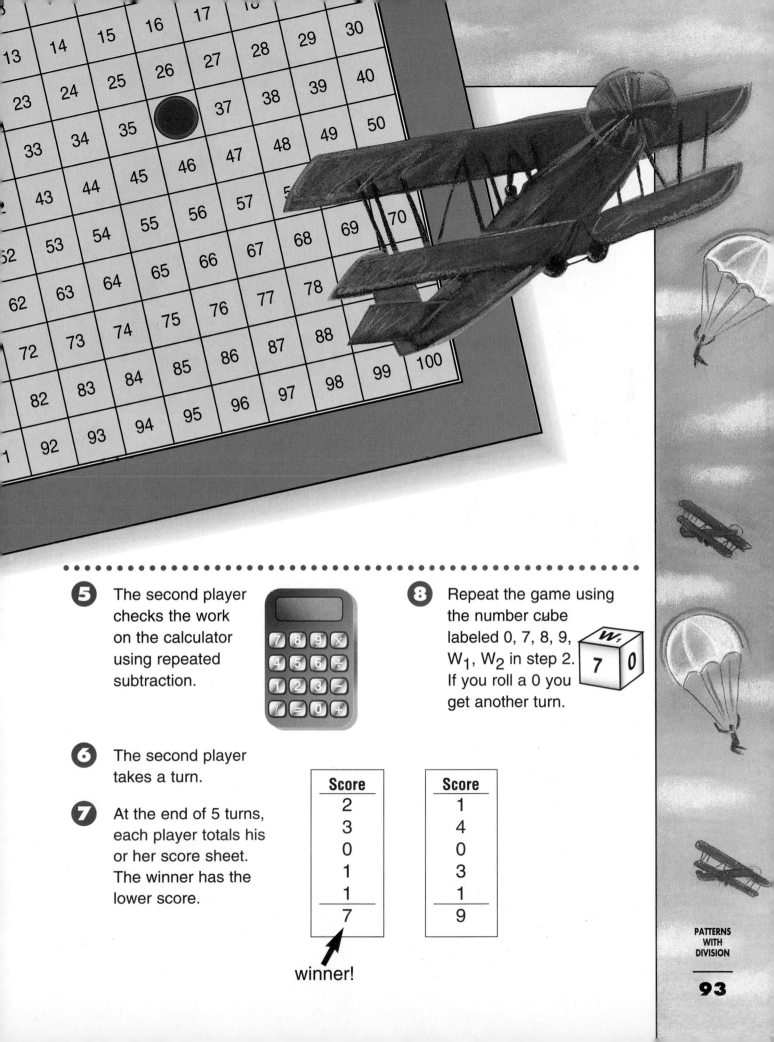

5 The second player checks the work on the calculator using repeated subtraction.

6 The second player takes a turn.

7 At the end of 5 turns, each player totals his or her score sheet. The winner has the lower score.

8 Repeat the game using the number cube labeled 0, 7, 8, 9, W_1, W_2 in step 2. If you roll a 0 you get another turn.

Score
2
3
0
1
1
7

winner!

Score
1
4
0
3
1
9

DESIGN YOUR OWN

Stamp Booklet

Amir's Plan

- ☐ shape — Square
- ☐ size — little
- ☐ color — red
- ☐ design — fire engine
- ☐ cost of stamp — 25¢
- ☐ layers — 5

Do you want all your stamps to look alike?

How many layers will you put in your booklet?

How much will each of your stamps cost?

How much will your booklet cost?

What will you put on the cover?

Have fun!

CheckYOURSELF

Great Job! Your stamp booklet shows an understanding of the concepts of multiplication and division. You used multiplication equations to show the number of stamps and to price your booklet. You used arrays as a model. You wrote clearly about your work.

Counting and Exchanging Money

*H*ow can we use money?

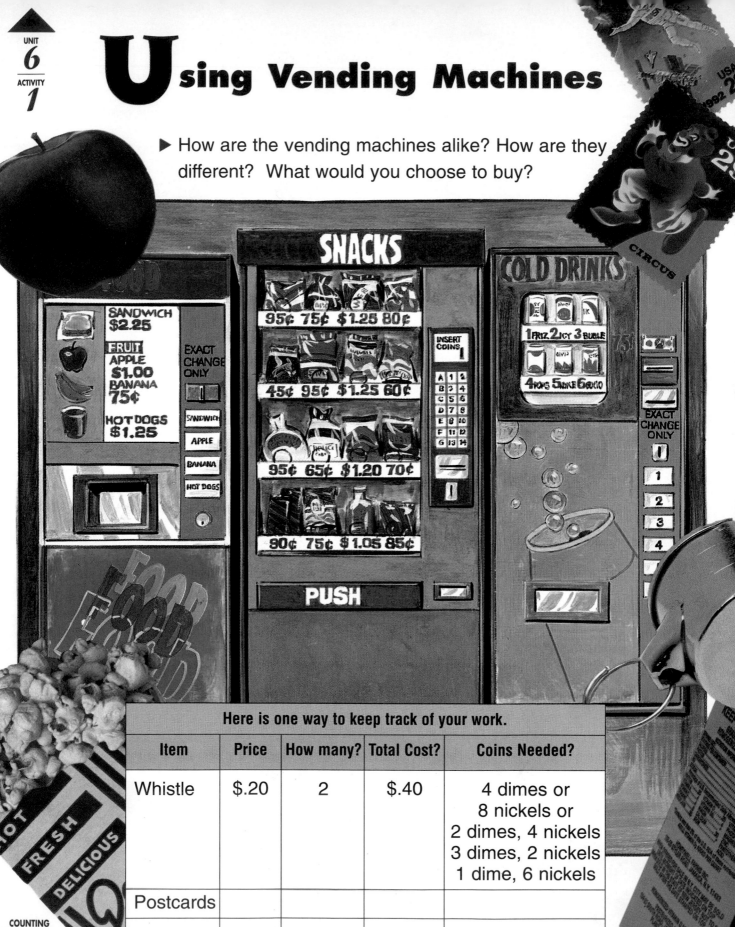

Using Vending Machines

▶ How are the vending machines alike? How are they different? What would you choose to buy?

SNACKS

95¢ 75¢ $1.25 80¢

45¢ 95¢ $1.25 60¢

95¢ 65¢ $1.20 70¢

90¢ 75¢ $1.05 85¢

INSERT COINS

PUSH

SANDWICH
$2.25

FRUIT
APPLE
$1.00
BANANA
75¢

HOT DOGS
$1.25

EXACT
CHANGE
ONLY

SANDWICH

APPLE

BANANA

HOT DOGS

COLD DRINKS

1 FRIZ 2 ICY 3 BUBLE

4 5 6

EXACT
CHANGE
ONLY

1
2
3
4

Here is one way to keep track of your work.

Item	Price	How many?	Total Cost?	Coins Needed?
Whistle	$.20	2	$.40	4 dimes or 8 nickels or 2 dimes, 4 nickels 3 dimes, 2 nickels 1 dime, 6 nickels
Postcards				

ON YOUR OWN

1. List all the different ways you can find to make $.40.

2. How many ways can you make $1.50 without using pennies, nickels, or dimes?

3. Look at the pile of coins. What trades would you make to get as many bills as possible? As few coins as possible? Explain.

| 9 quarters | 11 dimes | 11 nickels | 5 half-dollars | 12 pennies |

4. Ayesha has twice as many $1 bills as $5 bills. She has less than $20. How much money do you think she has? Explain.

5. Think about grocery store items you might find in your pantry, cupboard, or refrigerator that cost about $.50, about $1.00, about $2.50, and about $5.00. Guess two or three items for each price. Then check to see how close you were.

6. Figure out the value of each full roll of coins. Copy and complete the table.

Coin	Full Roll Has—	Value of Roll
penny	50	
nickel	40	
dime	50	
quarter	40	

7. *My Journal:* What have you learned about money?

UNIT 6 ACTIVITY 2

Mouth Watering Menus

Which menu contains more
mouth watering items?

What items would you order?

PASTA PASTA

GRANDE MEXICANA

BLACK BEAN SOUP	$1.95
TACO	2.50
BURRITO	3.75
CARNE ASADA	6.95
QUESADILLA	4.75
CHEESE ENCHILADA	3.50
CHICKEN ENCHILADA	3.75

SIDE ORDERS

TORTILLA CHIPS	$1.50
REFRIED BEANS	1.95
MEXICAN RICE	1.75
SALSA RANCHERA	1.95

DRINKS AND DESSERTS

MILK	$.75
FLAN	1.75

SALADS

Mixed Green	$3.25
Caesar Salad	4.75
Tomato & Cheese	4.25

PASTA

Spaghetti	$8.75
with Meatballs	10.95
Linguine with Clam Sauce	8.95
Fettuccine Alfredo	8.95
Ravioli	7.25
Lasagna	9.50
Chicken Parmesan	8.25
Pasta and Burger	6.95

DRINKS

Milk	$1.25
Fresh Juice	1.50
orange, apple, tomato	

GOLDEN DRAGON

Egg Roll	$1.25
Fried Wontons	1.95
Beef with Bean Cake	6.25
Beef with Broccoli	5.85
Chicken with Black Bean Sauce	6.95
Chicken with Pineapple	7.85
Egg Foo Young	4.25
Shrimp Lo Mein	6.70
Shrimp Fried Rice	4.25

SOUP

Egg Drop	$1.55
Chicken Noodle	1.75
Wonton	2.00

DRINKS

Milk	$1.35
Juice	1.10

DELI

Salads

GRILLED CHICKEN	$7.90
SPINACH	4.50

Sandwiches

HAMBURGER	$4.95
CHICKEN	7.50
TURKEY CLUB	7.50
BRISKET	7.95
BARBECUE	7.50

Dessert

KEY LIME PIE	$4.75
MUD PIE	3.50

Drinks

MILK	$1.00
JUICE	1.20

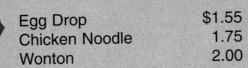

AMAZING
F A C T S

The Guinness Book of World Records *lists Tump Nak in Bangkok, Thailand, as the largest restaurant in the world. Tump Nak is 65 adjoining houses that cover a 10-acre area, giving the restaurant the capacity to serve 3,000 hungry customers.*

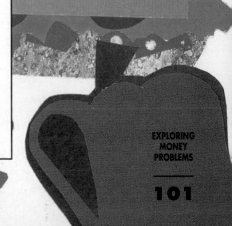

ON YOUR OWN

▶ Use the menus to answer these questions.

1. Why do foods at a restaurant cost more than the same food you might make at home?

2. If you had $7.00 to spend, which restaurant would give you the best choice for your money? Explain.

3. If you do not eat meat, which restaurant would you choose? Explain.

4. Choose one menu. Find the most expensive and least expensive items. What is the difference in cost between them? How does this compare with the most and least expensive items on the other menus?

5. If you had $30.00 to spend on a meal for your family members, which of these restaurants would you choose? Why? What foods would you order? Estimate the cost as you make up the order. Then find the exact cost and your change, if any.

6. *My Journal:* What did you like best about this activity? Why?

COWRIE SHELL MONEY

Have you ever wondered what kinds of money systems people used?

In many parts of the world people used beads and shells for money. Sometimes they would string beads and shells and wear money to show their wealth and have it handy.

One of the oldest forms of money dating back to ancient Africa, Asia and the South Pacific is the cowrie shell. Cowries are china-like oval shells about $1\frac{1}{2}$ inches long. The word cowrie comes from the Hindu *kauri*, meaning pearl.

In 17th century Africa 500 cowries bought a goat and 2 bought a chicken. In the early 19th century a house in India cost 16 million cowrie shells. Although cowrie shells are no longer used for money, they are still worn as jewelry and as decorations for clothes and hair.

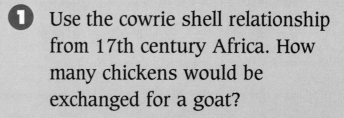

1 Use the cowrie shell relationship from 17th century Africa. How many chickens would be exchanged for a goat?

2 What do you think the seller of the house in 19th century India did with 16 million cowrie shells?

Currency Exchange

Travelers must trade the money they bring from home for the money used in the country they visit. They can trade money at some banks, airports, or hotels. Many cities also have places especially set up to trade money.

COUNTRY	U.S. $1 =
Canada	1.3 dollar
China	6 yuan
Ecuador	1895 sucre
Ghana	378 cedi
Guatemala	5 quetzal
India	31 rupee
Japan	107 yen
Kenya	29 shilling
Mexico	3 peso
Morocco	9 dirham
Philippines	28 peso
South Korea	810 won
Thailand	25 baht
Venezuela	94 bolivar

Now make a currency table of your own. Your teacher will give you the directions for your table.

CheckYOURSELF

Great Job! Your currency table shows the correct conversions for the amount you chose. You explained clearly in writing how and why the table works.

How can we measure length and area?

A Banquet!

How many tables are needed for 50 people?

Square card tables that seat one person on a side are going to be pushed together to make a long table. How many tables are needed to seat exactly 50 people?

How long is your arm span?

AMAZING
F A C T S

The tallest man for whom there are good recent records was Robert Wadlow. He was 8 feet 11 inches tall and had an arm span of 9 feet 5 $\frac{3}{4}$ inches!

ESTIMATING
AND
MEASURING
LENGTH

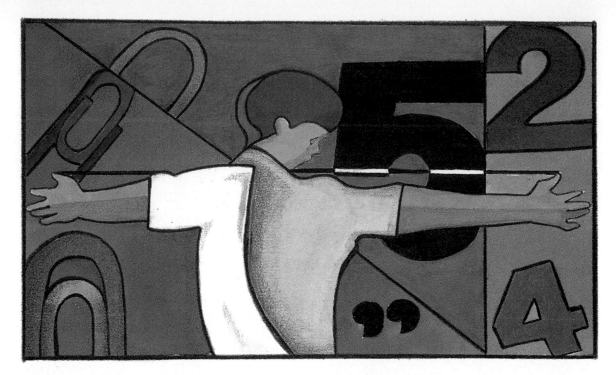

ON YOUR OWN

1. Draw a line shorter than your forearm, but longer than your foot. How long is your line?

2. Design a rectangular postcard. Make the sum of the lengths of the sides equal to 12 inches. Can you make more than one rectangle whose sides sum to 12 inches? Why did you choose yours?

3. How many children, lying on the floor and placed head to foot, would stretch from one end of your classroom to the other? Write how you would solve the problem without asking anyone to lie on the floor.

4. Decide which is longer. Write and share your reasoning.
   a. 5 chalk erasers placed end to end or the length of your desk
   b. 10 paper clips placed end to end or your foot
   c. height of the door or two classmates

5. Which pile would you rather have, an inch of nickels or a half-inch of quarters? Why?

6. *My Journal:* What have you learned about estimating length?

Are you a rectangle or a square?

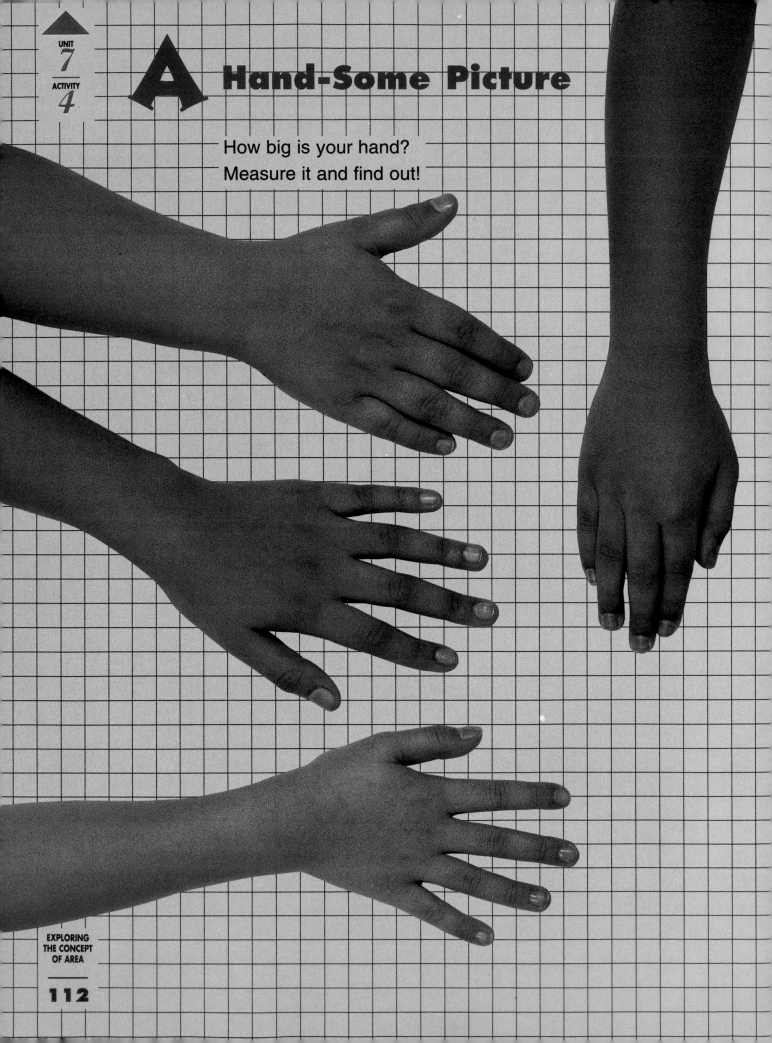

A Hand-Some Picture

How big is your hand?
Measure it and find out!

1. Guess how many square centimeters each of the following objects would cover:

a pencil, a floppy disk, a calculator, a key, a corn flake, a stamp, a leaf.

Now measure them on grid paper to check your estimate. Which was your closest guess?

2. Find an object that covers an area of about 10 square centimeters. Find one that you think is twice as big as that. Measure them to check your guesses.

3. Go on a Scavenger Hunt. Find and list objects that cover about 12 square centimeters, about 25 square centimeters, and about 50 square centimeters. Use centimeter grid paper to check your guesses.

4. *My Journal:* What did you find interesting about measuring the area of objects on grid paper?

EXPLORING
THE CONCEPT
OF AREA

Different Shapes, Same Area?

What is the area of each shape? Tell how you decided.

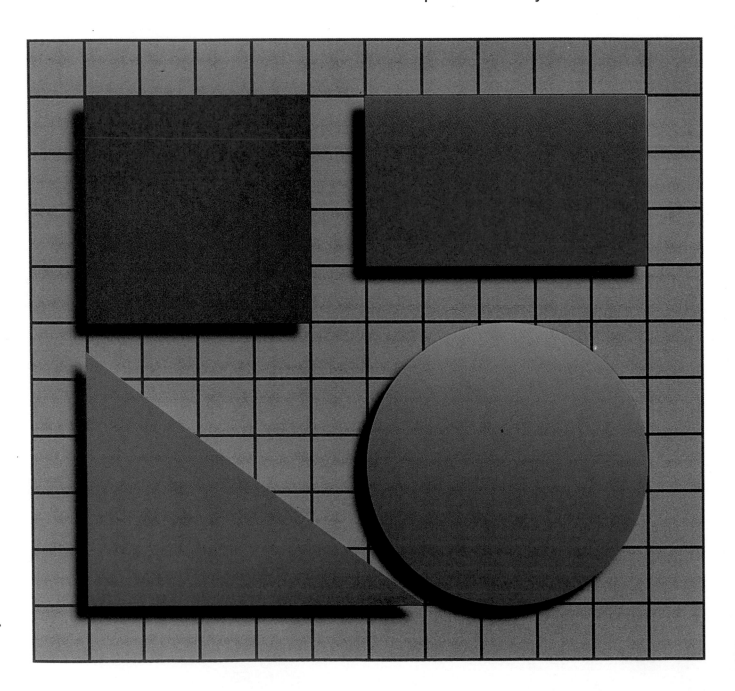

Can you draw different shapes that have about the same area?

At Arms

Have you ever wondered how people measured before tools and instruments like we use were available?

People around the world used what was readily available. The Egyptians used units based on finger, hand, and arm lengths.

Centuries ago people in England used a system much like the Egyptian one. It too was based on finger, hand and arm lengths. Both systems were based on tens. The chart shows some of the units.

1 What systems do both Egypt and England use today? What number is it based on?

2 Make up your own system based on fingers, hands, and arms. Decide if it should be based on tens.

Measure	Egypt	England
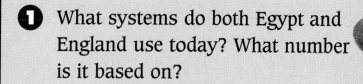 fingerwidth	zebo	fingerwidth
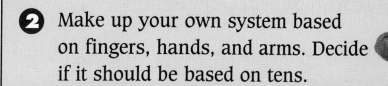 ten zebos or fingerwidths	span	span-of-length
ten spans	nent	armstretch or fathom
ten nents or fathoms	khet	chain

The Big Coverup

First, make an estimate. Then measure!

Item Measured Unit of Area Estimate Measurement

envelope   square cm   250 square cm 325 square cm

You will need centimeter grid paper.

1. Do you think a rectangle and a square with the same perimeter have the same area? Write what you think and why. Show examples if you can.

2. Draw a rectangle that has a perimeter of 12. Draw a square next to it that has a perimeter of 12. Then tell the area of each. Use grid paper if you like.

3. On grid paper, draw as many rectangles with different lengths and widths as you can that have an area of 20 square centimeters. Tell the perimeter of each.

4. *My Journal:* What do you know about area? Tell what is easy and what is difficult for you in working with area.

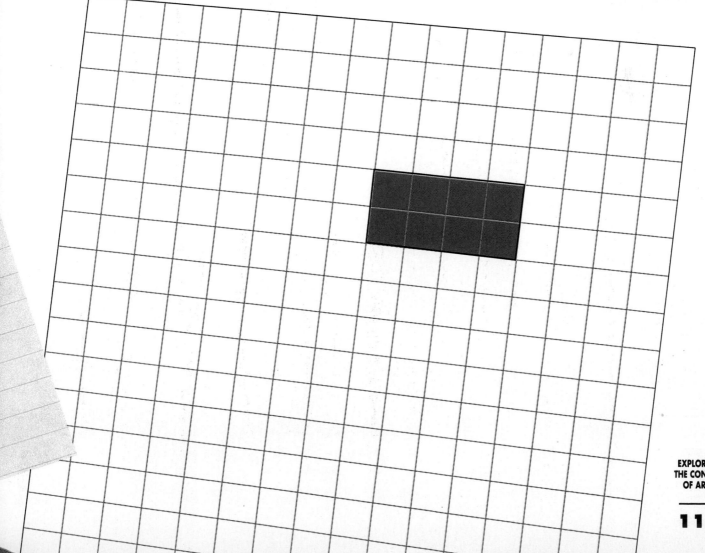

When Is an Estimate Good Enough?

Read each situation below. Talk about it and decide if estimating the solution makes sense or if an actual measurement is needed. Explain your decision.

1. You are filling cups for customers at your lemonade stand. You want to give each person about the same amount of lemonade.

2. You need to know the size of your foot for new sneakers.

3. You are designing the frog jump pit for the Amazing Pet Contest.

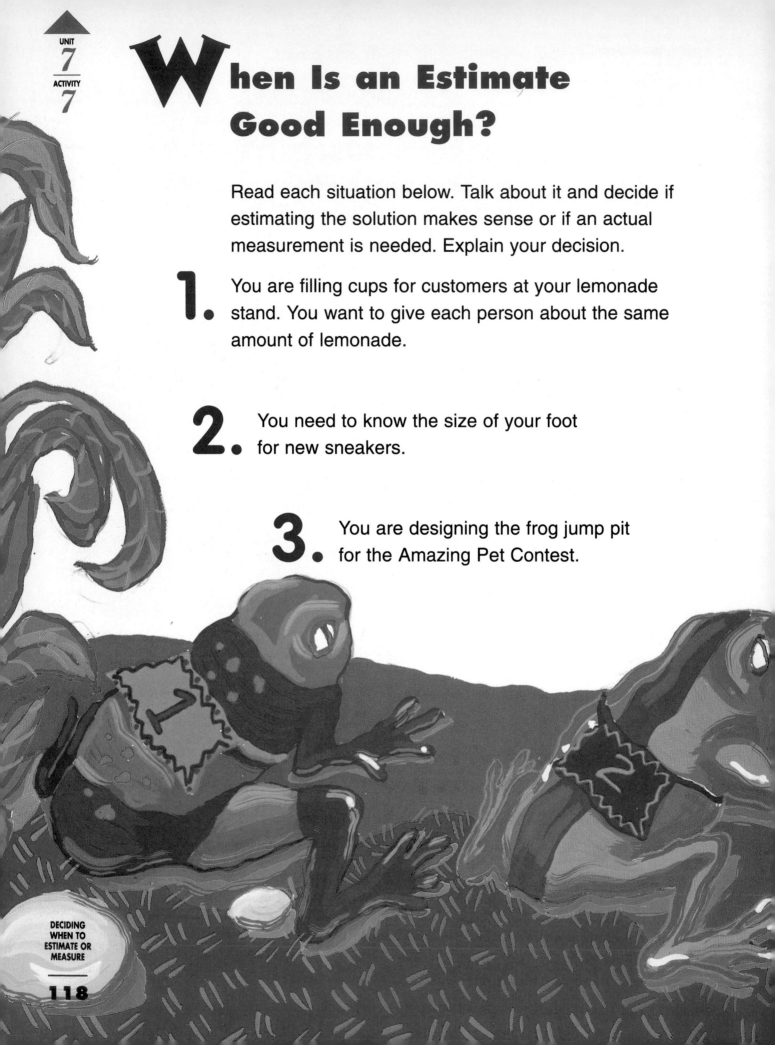

DECIDING
WHEN TO
ESTIMATE OR
MEASURE

4. You are buying fabric to make eight skirts for dancers in a performance.

5. You need a box big enough to hold all your dinosaur models.

6. You are cutting out letters for a sign. You want all of them to be the same height.

7. You are going to ride your bicycle to a birthday party. You need to figure out when to leave.

8. You are making a frame for a photo you are giving to your friend on his or her birthday.

9. You are making a fancy, delicate dessert for a party!

Have a Measuring OLYMPICS

You and your group will have one of these events to plan. You will create the rules for winning and judging the event. You will also make a recording sheet for scoring the event.

Event 1: PACE-UP

Pick a starting line close to the back of the classroom. Estimate how many steps it will take you to reach the front wall. Record your estimate and the actual number of steps.

Event 2: SWIM RELAY

Start at the wall. Walk a distance you estimate to be 10 feet. Put a marker there. Measure to check. Repeat 5 times.

Event 3: TOSS UP

Place a Link-it on the ground. Stand back 3 paces. Toss a counter or a coin at the Link-it. Estimate how close you get to it. Measure to check.

Event 4: PLAN A POOL

On a centimeter grid, draw a pool shape that you estimate to have an area of 50 centimeter squares. Check your estimate.

Event 5: RECTANGLE UNTANGLE

Estimate to draw a rectangle that has twice the area of a rectangle a member of another team draws on grid paper. Check your estimate.

Event 6: SCHOOL WALK

Estimate the number of paces it would take you to walk around your school. Check your estimate.

Check YOURSELF

Your plans for your event were well-organized. You created a good recording sheet for the event and helped to make sure that the rules for winning were clear and fair. You wrote to explain how length and area were used in the events in the Measuring Olympics.

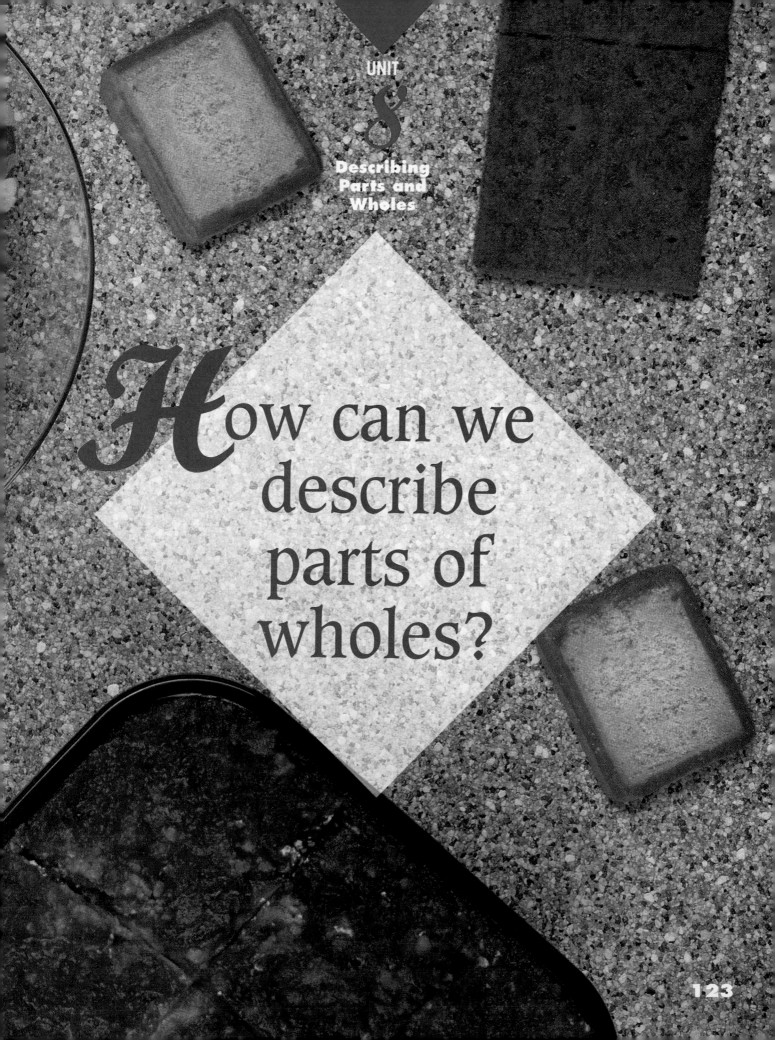

How can we describe parts of wholes?

Make it Fair!

Fractions name equal parts of wholes.

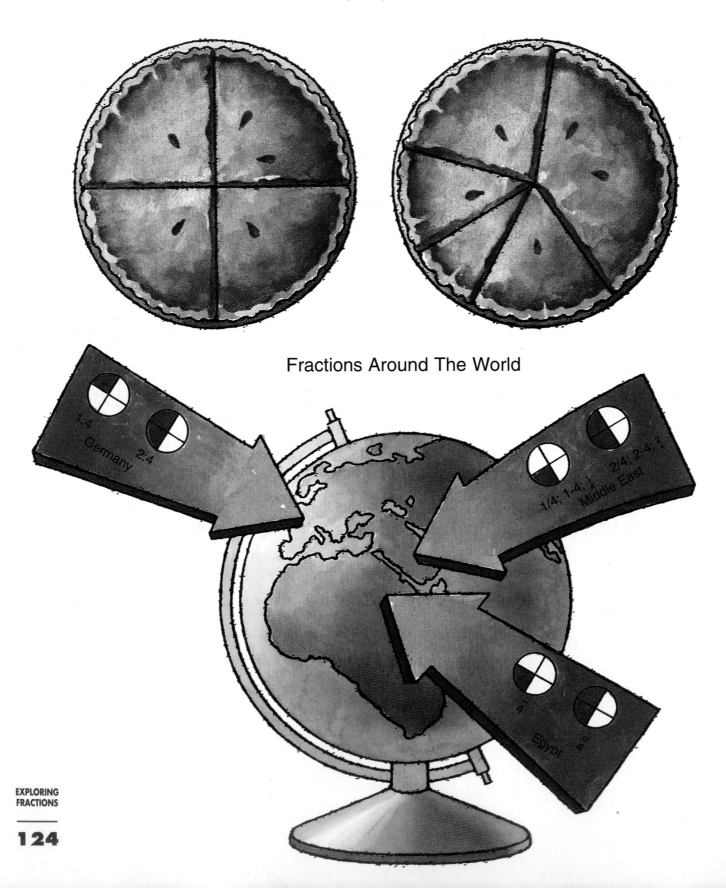

Fractions Around The World

Covering Up

Which block can be used repeatedly to cover this design?

Can you find another block that also can be used to completely cover the design?

▶ Try to cover each shape with as many different types of blocks as possible. Use only one color at a time. For each type that you use, write a fraction that describes what part of the whole each block covers.

 1

2

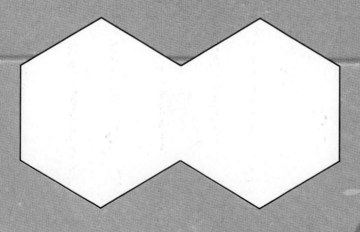

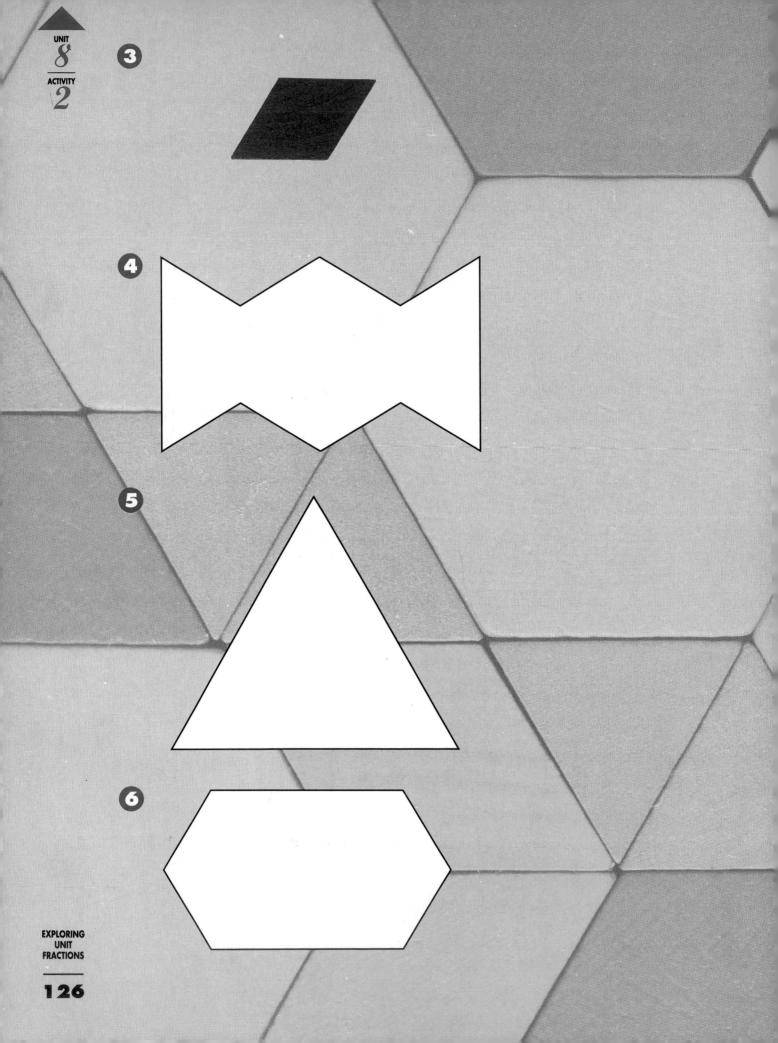

③

④

⑤

⑥

1. The shape below represents $\frac{1}{4}$ of the whole unit. Draw a picture that shows what the whole might look like.

2. Use the same shape as in Problem 1, but now let it represent $\frac{1}{3}$. Draw a picture that shows what the whole might look like.

3. Look at the design below. Give two fractions that name what part of the whole the trapezoid covers.

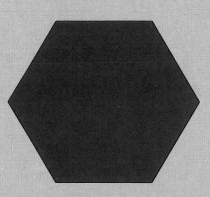

4. Make any design using Power Polygon shapes. Write and tell what fraction each type of polygon is of the whole.

5. *My Journal:* What did you learn that was new?

Going Halves

How many ways can you make a half?
Compare the halves you have made.

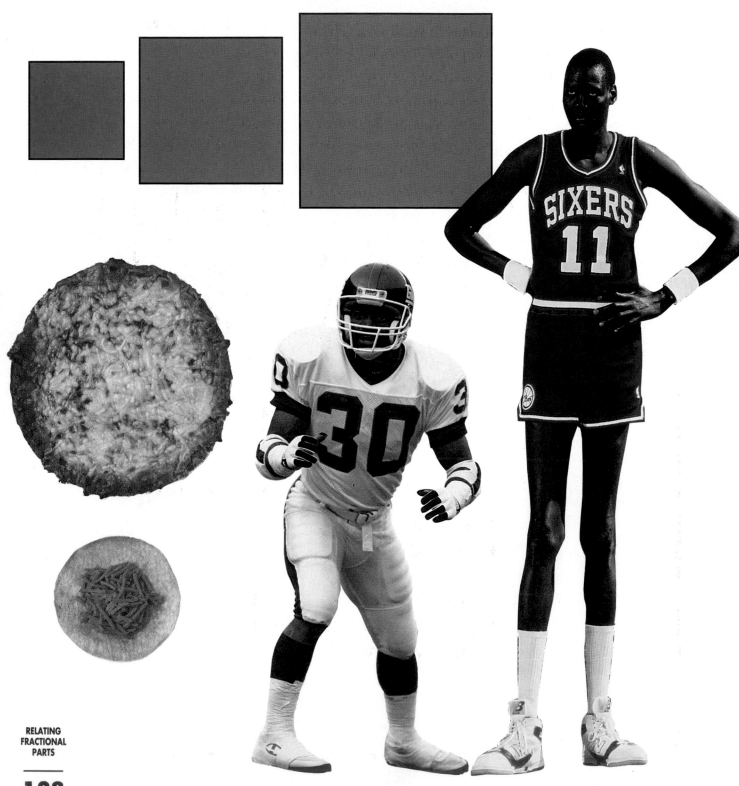

LOOK TO THE TREES

Did you ever wonder where in the real world you would find fractions?

Just look at some trees around you. The branches, buds and flowers are arranged in circular spirals. The fraction tells you how far around the branch to go. Scientist Boris A. Kordemsky recorded the fractions for certain trees.

linden and elm	$\frac{1}{2}$
beech	$\frac{1}{3}$
oak and cherry	$\frac{2}{5}$
poplar and pear	$\frac{3}{8}$

Notice that the circles spiral up.

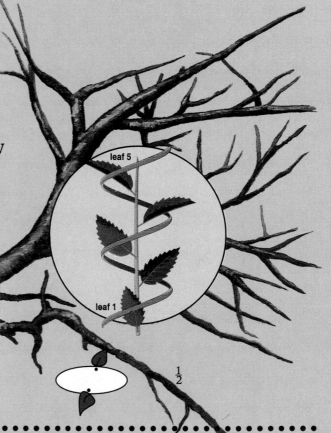

leaf 5

leaf 1

$\frac{1}{2}$

1 Draw a circular diagram for the leaves on a beech or an oak tree.

2 Look at a tree branch with leaves. Draw the leaves on a circle. Write a fraction for the part of the circle between two leaves.

Fold and Fold Again

▶ Folding Halves

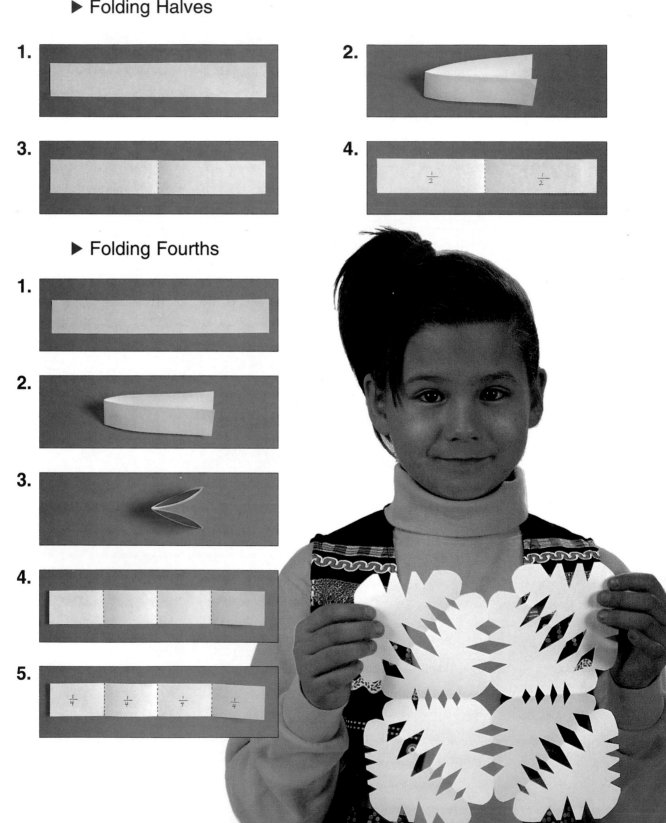

1.

2.

3.

4. $\frac{1}{2}$ $\frac{1}{2}$

▶ Folding Fourths

1.

2.

3.

4.

5. $\frac{1}{4}$ $\frac{1}{4}$ $\frac{1}{4}$ $\frac{1}{4}$

Fraction Reaction

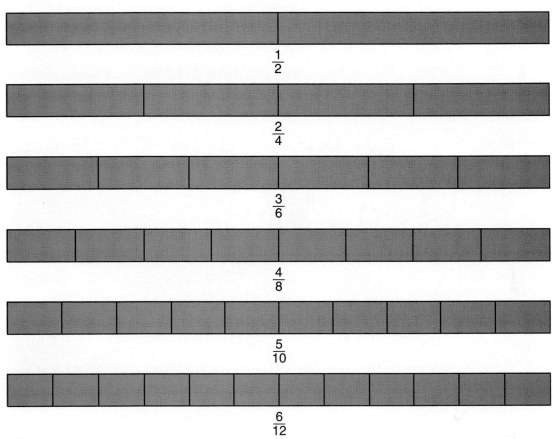

$\frac{1}{2}$

$\frac{2}{4}$

$\frac{3}{6}$

$\frac{4}{8}$

$\frac{5}{10}$

$\frac{6}{12}$

ON YOUR OWN

1. Lila drew the picture below. She then concluded that $\frac{1}{2}$ is equivalent to $\frac{1}{3}$. Is she correct or incorrect? Write explaining why.

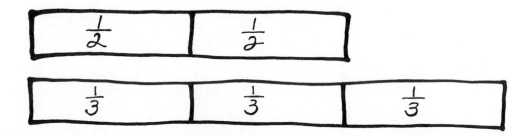

| $\frac{1}{2}$ | $\frac{1}{2}$ | |
| $\frac{1}{3}$ | $\frac{1}{3}$ | $\frac{1}{3}$ |

2. *My Journal:* What did you find interesting about the activity?

EQUIVALENT
FRACTIONS
USING STRIPS

A Good Diet

Do the pictures in each pair show the same amount?

1 I'll ONLY Eat 1 PiEce and SAVE RoOm For DessErt.

2 I'll ONLY EaT 3 not 6!

I'll be luckier! I HAVe 6 ChaNces to win!

Solve each problem.

1. You cut a piece of ribbon into 4 equal pieces. How can you now cut the ribbon to get pieces that are $\frac{1}{8}$ of the whole piece?

2. If you cut the ribbon to make 8 pieces, can you cut it again to get pieces that are $\frac{1}{10}$ of the whole piece? Explain.

3. You bake two same size cakes. Your friends ate $\frac{2}{3}$ of one cake. You cut the other cake into 6 equal slices. How many slices would your friends have to eat to match what they ate from the first cake? Explain.

4. Copy the figure shown at the right. Color $\frac{8}{10}$ of it red. Write another fraction with a smaller denominator to describe the part you colored. Draw a picture or use a fraction strip to prove your answer is correct.

5. *My Journal:* What do you know about equivalent fractions? Do you feel that finding equivalent fractions is easy or hard? Why?

Making MATCHES

7	1	2	3	4	5	6
14	8	9	10	11	12	13
21	15	16	17	18	19	20
28	22	23	24	25	26	27
	29	30				

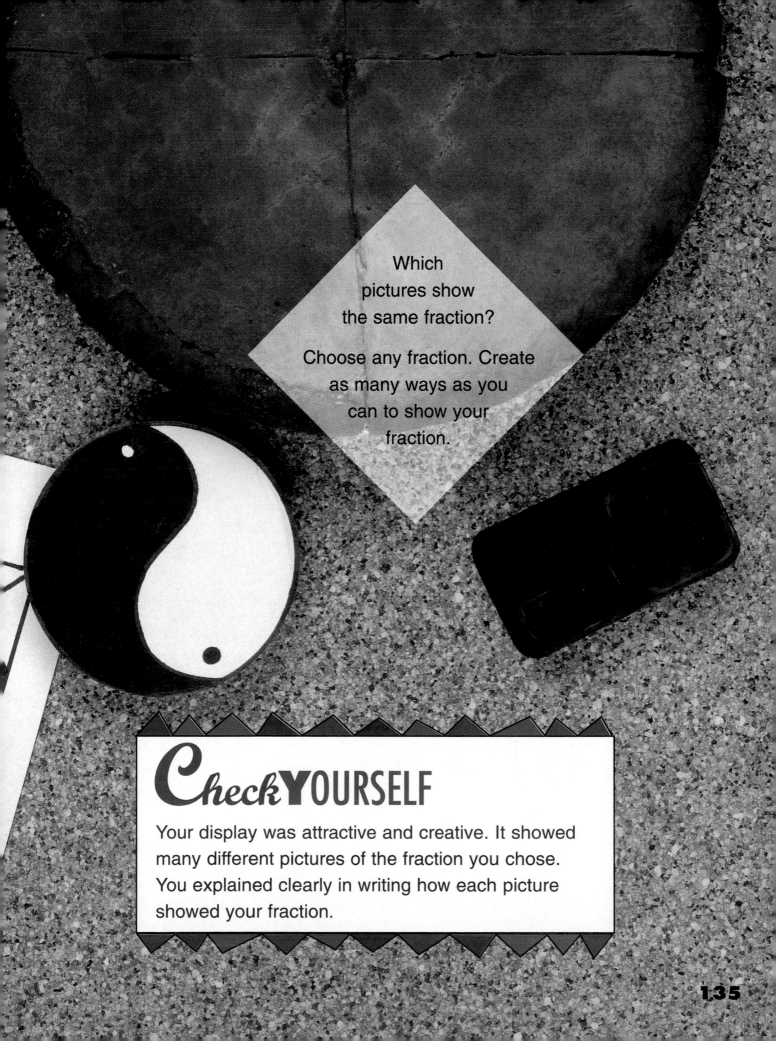

Which pictures show the same fraction?

Choose any fraction. Create as many ways as you can to show your fraction.

Check**Y**OURSELF

Your display was attractive and creative. It showed many different pictures of the fraction you chose. You explained clearly in writing how each picture showed your fraction.

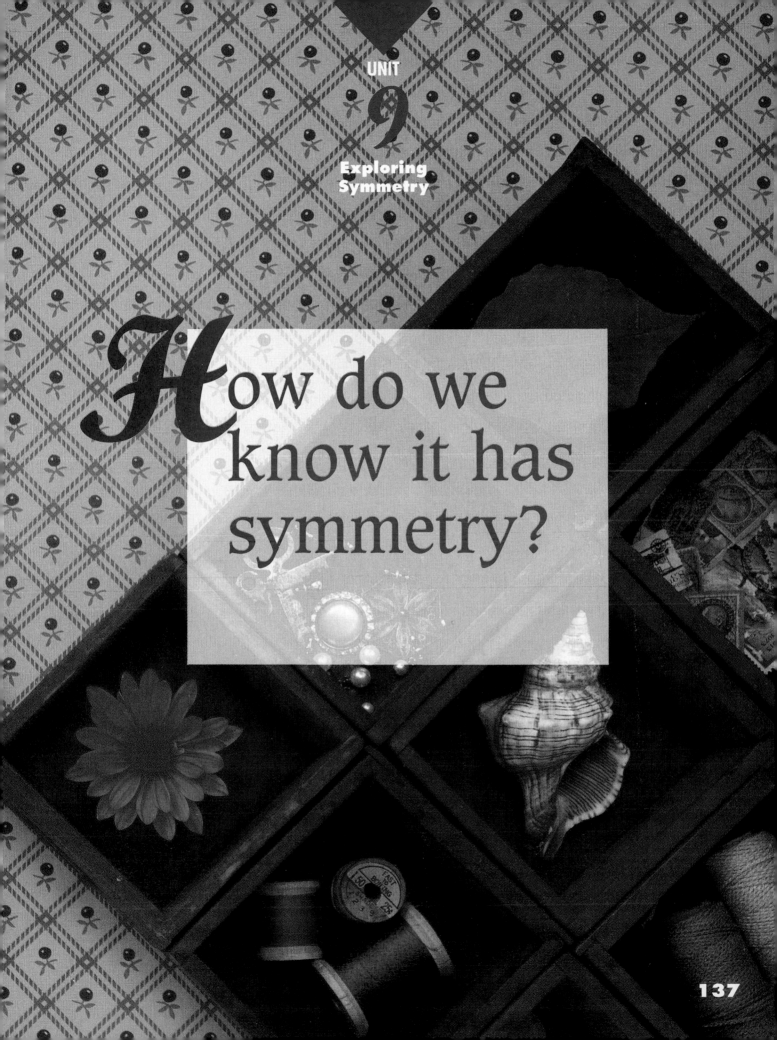

*H*ow do we know it has symmetry?

Find the Line!

ON
YOUR
OWN

1. Think about objects that have line symmetry. Why do you think many things people build are designed to have line symmetry?

2. Do numbers have line symmetry? Make a chart to show what you can discover about symmetry in the digits 0 to 9. Are the findings true for the kind of digits used in a calculator display? Explain.

3. Where can you find line symmetry on your own body? Describe and draw three examples. Show where to find the line(s) of symmetry.

4. *My Journal:* Tell what you know about line symmetry. Draw pictures to support your ideas.

Halve a Heart

▶ Copy and complete the designs so that they are symmetrical.

ON YOUR OWN

1. Follow the steps to make Happy Hound. You need 2 square pieces of paper.

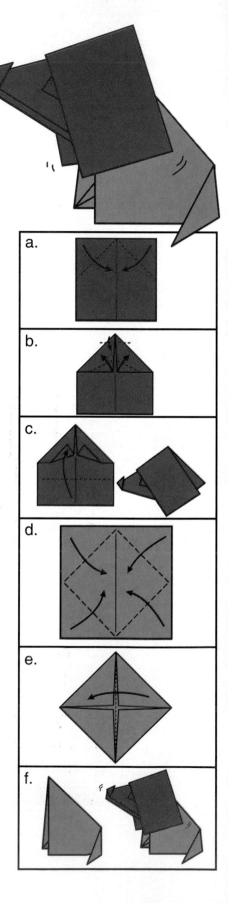

- First make Happy Hound's head. Start with one square of paper.

   a. Fold the paper in half. Unfold. Now fold each top corner to the middle.

   b. Fold up center corners a little. This makes eyes. Fold down the top center corner a little. This makes a nose.

   c. Fold the bottom up to the folded eyes. Fold the head in half. Do you see the ears, nose, and eyes? Put the head aside for now.

- Next make Happy Hound's body. Use the other square of paper.

   d. Fold paper in half. Unfold. Now fold each corner to the middle.

   e. Fold the new shape in half along the original fold you made in step d.

   f. Fold in the bottom corner to make a tail.

   Balance the head on top of the pointed neck. Gently pet Happy Hound. Watch her head bounce!

2. Copy each figure onto dot paper. Then complete each one so that when you unfold the paper, the figure is symmetrical. The fold is the line of symmetry.

a. **b.** **c.**

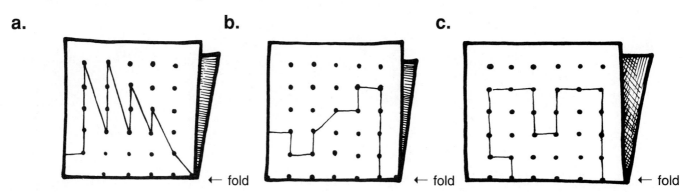

← fold   ← fold   ← fold

3. Copy each figure onto grid paper. Then complete each one so that when you unfold the paper, the figure is symmetrical. The fold is the line of symmetry.

a. **b.** **c.**

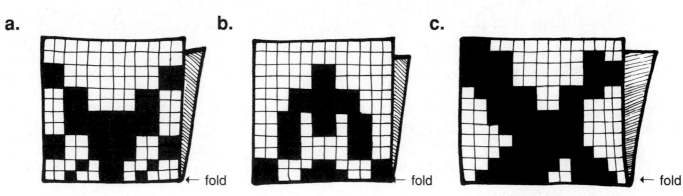

← fold   ← fold   ← fold

4. Use dot paper or grid paper. Create a design as complicated as you wish but it must have one or more lines of symmetry.

5. Make a symmetric design. Draw it, fold it, or use any materials you have. Write to describe how you made your design. Tell how you know it has line symmetry.

6. *My Journal:* Describe line symmetry in your own words. Tell why it is important.

Repeat YOURSELF

Did you ever wonder how people use symmetry?

Symmetry is in designs of all kinds in nature and in designs people have made.

Some examples of symmetry in nature are:

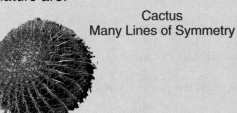

Cactus
Many Lines of Symmetry

Starfish
5 Lines of Symmetry

Rubber Plant Leaf
1 Line of Symmetry

Symmetric designs made by people include:

Aztec Goddess
1 Line of Symmetry

Persian Rug
2 Lines of Symmetry

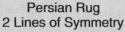

1 Why do you think people from different parts of the world use symmetry in their designs?

2 Find some symmetric designs that interest you in objects in your home, fabrics, pictures in magazines, or in nature. Tell how many lines of symmetry each example has.

3 Make your own symmetric design. Tell what you would use it for.

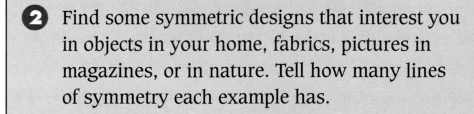

Symmetric Designs Plus

ON YOUR OWN

1. Use any materials you have at home to create a symmetric design with at least two lines of symmetry. Bring it to class. Ask a classmate to find the lines of symmetry.

2. Find three objects in your home that have line symmetry. Describe or draw each and tell where to find its lines of symmetry.

3. Find three objects in your neighborhood that have line symmetry. Describe or draw each and tell where to find its lines of symmetry.

4. Look at the thunderbird. You can find this symbol in some American Indian art, especially in the Pacific Northwest. Does it have symmetry? If so, how many lines of symmetry are there? Describe what you see.

5. Design a symbol to stand for yourself, your school, your town, or your family. Make it have one or more lines of symmetry.

6. *My Journal:* In what situations might you be interested in using line symmetry? Explain.

Snowflakes come in many, many shapes, but no one has ever found two that are exactly alike. Most unbroken snowflakes have line symmetry. All natural snowflakes, which are formed from crystals of ice, have six sides.

Follow these steps.

1. Design two Power Polygons puzzles. Make one that has no lines of symmetry and another that has 1 or more lines of symmetry. Record the way you used the shape to make your puzzle.

2. Trace just the outline of each puzzle on drawing paper. On the back, tell how many lines of symmetry the puzzle has, and describe where the lines are. Include other clues if you want.

3. Exchange puzzles with a classmate. Try to use the Pattern Blocks Plus pieces to make the puzzle.

4. When you think you have solved the puzzle, ask the puzzle maker to check. If you find a correct, but different solution, trace it to share later, and try again. Keep trying until you find the original solution.

This puzzle was drawn
on triangular dot paper.
It uses 8 pieces and has
1 line of symmetry.

Checklist for Making a Puzzle	**Checklist for Solving a Puzzle**
• How many lines of symmetry will your puzzle have? • Is your puzzle interesting and challenging? • How many pieces will you use? • How can you record your puzzle? • What clues can you give the solver?	• How many lines of symmetry must you think about? Where can they be? • What other clues did the puzzle maker give you? • What do you know about the pieces that can help you? • What other hints would help?

*C*heck**Y**OURSELF

You created two good puzzles, one without
symmetry and one with at least 1 line of symmetry.
Your clues were helpful, but did not give too much
away. You wrote to explain how you used symmetry
and various shapes to make your puzzle.

How can we multiply using arrays?

Photo Finish

Ways with Arrays

3 x 17 = ?

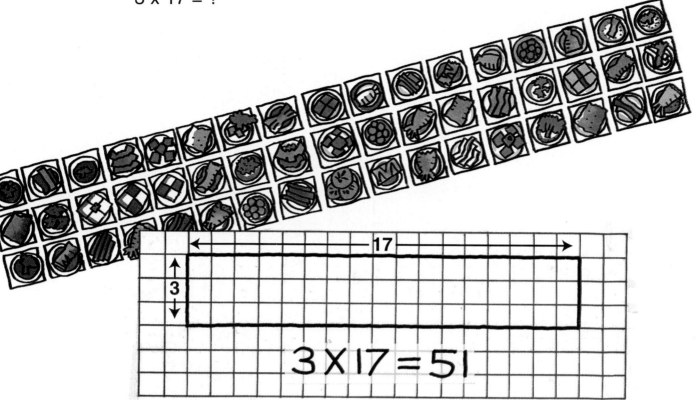

$$3 \times 17 = 51$$

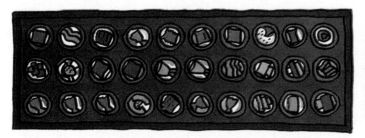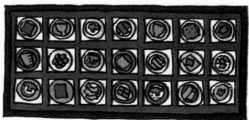

$$3 \times 17 = 51$$

Which array of blocks uses fewer blocks? Why?

ON YOUR OWN

▶ Write a multiplication problem. Find the total.

1.

2.

3. Find an array at home. Write a multiplication problem for it. Draw a picture to show your solution.

4. *My Journal:* What difficulties have you had working with large arrays? What could help?

Solve a Simpler Problem

In the subway station there was a 13 by 22 tile space to be filled. Here are some artists' designs:

Red, Red, Red
by Carmen

Land and Sky
by Ima Cloud

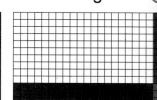
Flag
by A. Banner

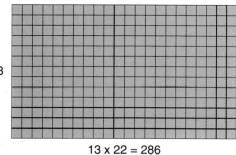
22
13
13 x 22 = 286

This shows that
13 x 22 = 286.

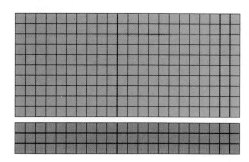

This also shows 286. Write a multiplication equation for each part. How can you find the total?

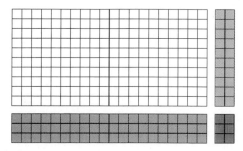

This shows 286, too. Write a multiplication equation for each part. How can you find the total?

► What is the total number of blocks? How did you find it?

1.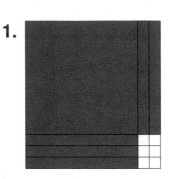

2.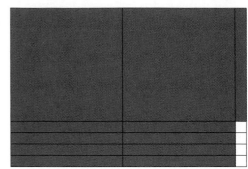

3. Use two pieces of grid paper. On one piece, draw a rectangle that shows a large number multiplication equation. On the other piece, make the same rectangle, then cut it up to show partial products. Write a multiplication equation for each.

4. Jevon wanted to multiply 2 x 14.

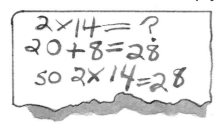

Draw a picture that might explain Jevon's thinking.

5. Draw a picture of a base ten block rectangle for 12 x 14. Use different colors for 8, 20, 40, and 100.

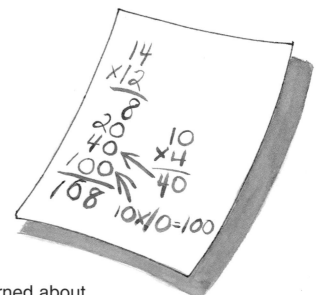

6. *My Journal:* What have you learned about multiplying larger numbers and partial products that you didn't know before?

Missing Sides

Willy is making crossword puzzles. He has 300 same size squares that he wants to put into 12 rows. How many go in each row?

12 rows

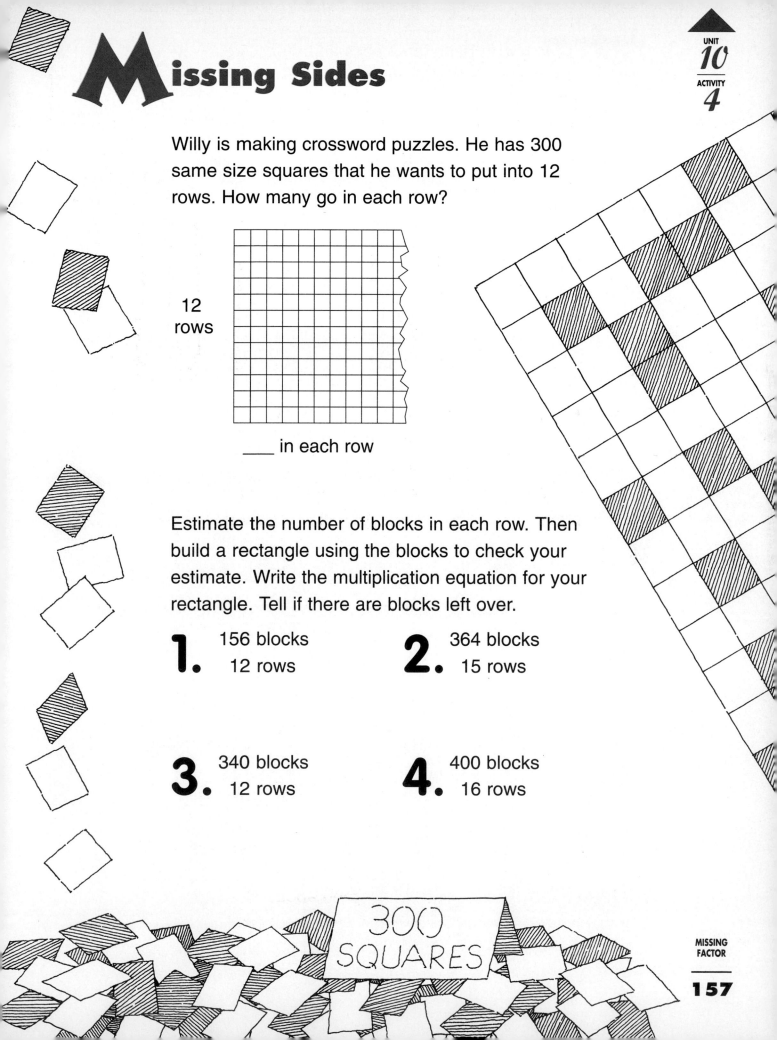

___ in each row

Estimate the number of blocks in each row. Then build a rectangle using the blocks to check your estimate. Write the multiplication equation for your rectangle. Tell if there are blocks left over.

1. 156 blocks
12 rows

2. 364 blocks
15 rows

3. 340 blocks
12 rows

4. 400 blocks
16 rows

300 SQUARES

ON YOUR OWN

▶ Use base ten blocks and grid paper to help you solve Problems 1-5.

1. Start with 250 blocks. How many in each row if there are 10 rows? 12 rows? 15 rows? Use words or pictures to show your solutions.

2. How many blocks must you start with to build a rectangle with 12 rows and have 5 left over? Give as many different answers as you can.

3. A minivan holds 15 students and costs $89.95, including tax, to rent for 1 day. What is the total cost to rent vans for 275 students for 1 day?

4. Ruby used 147 blocks. She made a rectangle with 14 rows. How can you know whether she had any blocks left over? Prove your answer.

5. Draw your own array, label one side and the number of blocks in all. Tell how you can find the missing side.

6. *My Journal:* What have you learned about missing sides and how to find them?

MISSING FACTOR

Making Arrangements

Here is 96.

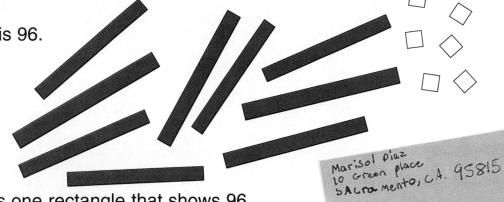

Here's one rectangle that shows 96.

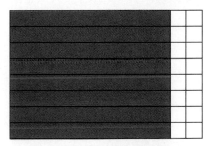

Here's another rectangle that shows 96.

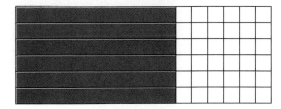

Do you think there are any others?

How would you find out?
Use as few blocks as possible.

Marisol Diaz
10 Green place
Sacramento, CA. 95815

Trish Gorman
1526 Oak St. Apt.3
Peekskill, N.y. 10566

Sean Reilly
157 Cabrillo Blvd.
Oklahoma City, Ok. 73105

Jack Plc
34 over
Cincinn

Ms. C. Jones
4601 9th Street
Seattle, WA. 98121

The first &
2629 Perry Bl
San Diego, CA

1. Write a multiplication equation to fit the pictures.

a.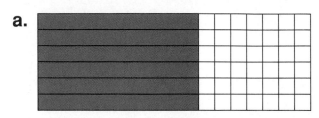

b.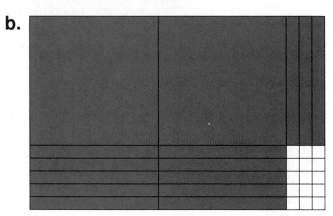

2. Draw the rectangle. Write a multiplication equation for the total.

   a. The factors are 13 and 8.

   b. The factors are 26 and 14.

3. Pick two factors. One could be your age. Let the other be any 2-digit number. Show how to find the product.

4. Break apart the rectangle to write multiplication equations for the total.

   a.    b.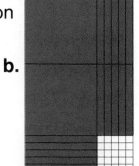

5. Find the missing factor.

a.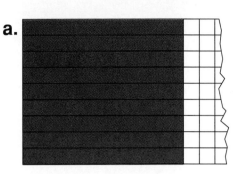

The total is 162.

b.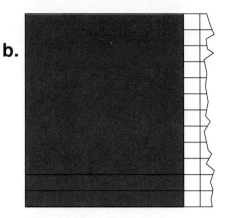

The total is 216.

6. Make at least two rectangles. Write an equation for each.
   a. The total is 144.
   b. The total is 360.

7. Pick a number. Make a rectangle for that number. Draw it on grid paper. Write a multiplication equation for it.

8. What does it mean when you can't make a rectangle with a given side and a given total number of blocks? Use a side of 21 blocks and a total of 150 blocks to explain.

9. *My Journal:* What do you think about to help you find missing factors?

DOUBLES or LATTICE work?

Have you ever wondered if other people developed procedures for multiplication different from those you and your classmates have worked out?

The lattice method of multiplication is believed to have been used first in India. Chinese, Arabs, and Persians all favored this method. The method found its way into Italian texts in the 14th century.

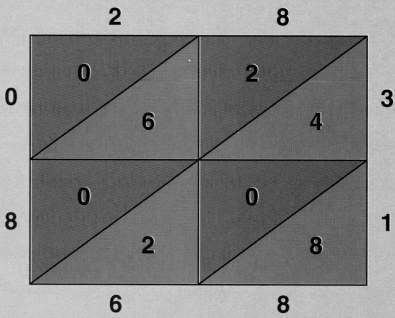

❶ What is the product of 8 and 3? of 8 and 1? of 2 and 3? of 2 and 1?

❷ Can you find each product on the lattice?

❸ Then find the sum of the numbers on each diagonal.

The doubles or duplication
method of multiplication was
used by the Egyptians and a
version of this method is still
used in Russia today.

1 • 28 = 28

2 • 28 = 56

4 • 28 = 112

8 • 28 = 224

16 • 28 = 448
——————————
31 • 28 = 868

4 Using the duplication method, how would
you find 7 x 28?

5 Find the product of 15 and 27 using
duplication.

6 How do people you know multiply?

Telling Times

What is each pair doing?

AMAZING
F A C T S

Mrs. Shakuntala Devi of India has developed her own fast way to multiply. It took her only 28 seconds of mental math to find the product of two 13-digit numbers!

ON YOUR OWN

▶ Solve each problem. Explain your solution in writing.

1. "I have $5.50. Can I buy 3 boxes?"

SALE! PASQUALE'S PASTA $1.79

2. "Which box is a better buy?"

SUDZ $5.99 washes 42 loads

$2.99 KLEENE washes 24 loads

3. "One can serves 4 people. I'm serving 42 people. How many cans should I buy?"

Fruit Cocktail

4. "I have $15. How many dinners can I buy?"

Mr. Big $2.09 Dinners

MR BIG FROZEN DINNER

MR BIG FROZEN DIN

5. In what kinds of situations can you picture yourself multiplying and dividing? Give two examples.

6. Choose two two-digit numbers. Find their product using your own procedure.

7. *My Journal:* What do you like about multiplying larger numbers? What did you find easy to do?

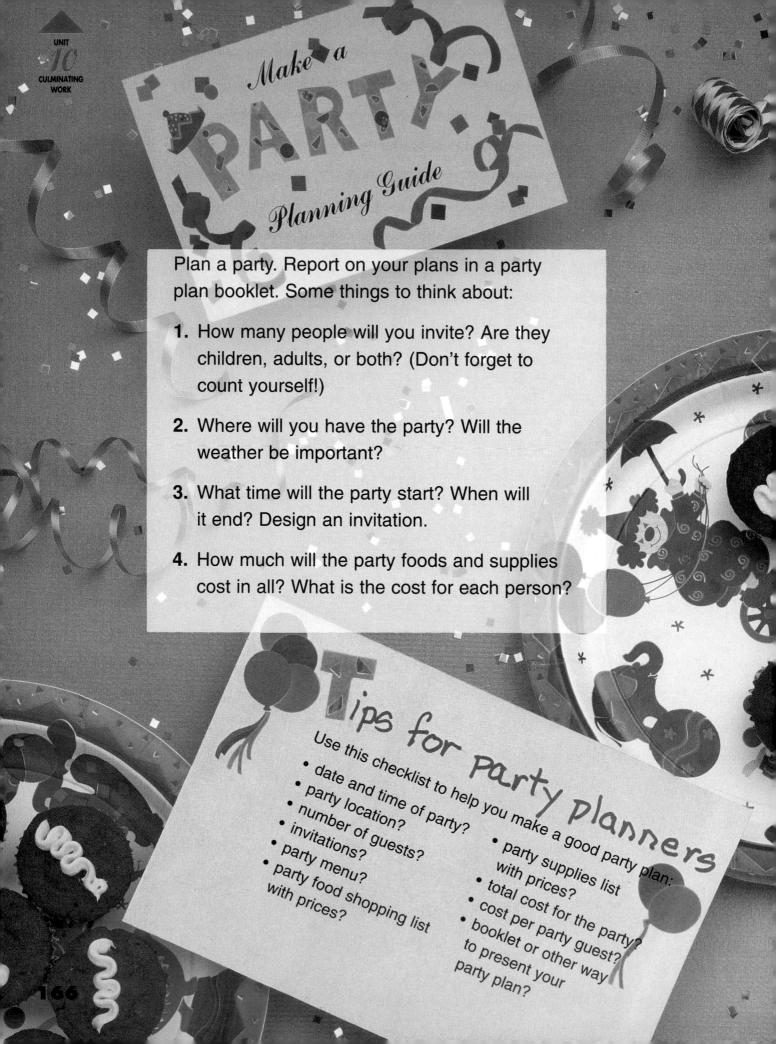

Make a

PARTY

Planning Guide

Plan a party. Report on your plans in a party plan booklet. Some things to think about:

1. How many people will you invite? Are they children, adults, or both? (Don't forget to count yourself!)

2. Where will you have the party? Will the weather be important?

3. What time will the party start? When will it end? Design an invitation.

4. How much will the party foods and supplies cost in all? What is the cost for each person?

Tips for party planners

Use this checklist to help you make a good party plan:

- date and time of party?
- party location?
- number of guests?
- invitations?
- party menu?
- party food shopping list with prices?
- party supplies list with prices?
- total cost for the party?
- cost per party guest?
- booklet or other way to present your party plan?

Use the data in this chart to help you make choices about food for your party. You can also look through store ads. Think about which size item you'll need.

Item	Size	Servings	Cost
Cake	small large	12 slices 24 slices	$3.97 $7.50
Cheese	medium large	16 slices 24 slices	$2.89 $4.44
Fruit cocktail	small large	8 people 20 people	$1.99 $3.59
Hamburgers	1 pound	3 burgers	$1.77
Hamburger buns	regular family size	8 buns 16 buns	$1.25 $2.09
Ice cream	small large	5 scoops 14 scoops	$1.77 $4.29
Ketchup	regular bottle	20 servings	$1.67
Milk	quart gallon	4 servings 16 servings	$0.85 $ 2.33
Pizza	small pie large pie	6 slices 8 slices	$7.50 $9.00
Potato salad	regular container	4 servings	$1.33
Juice	6-pack	6 bottles	$2.39

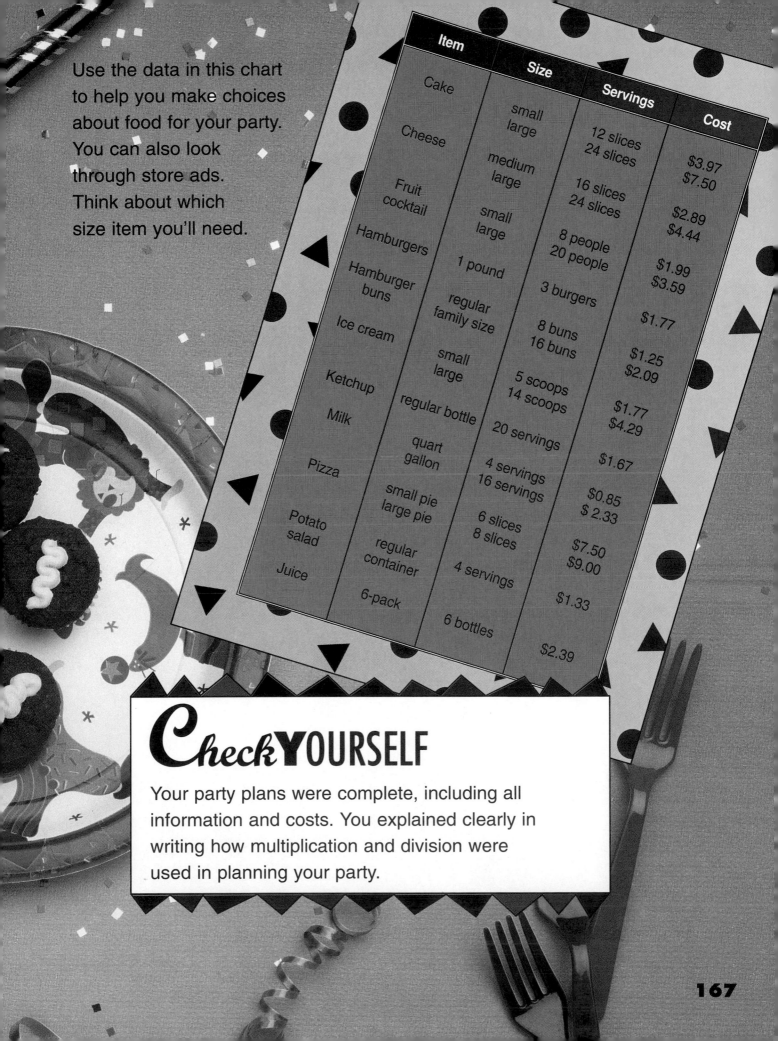

Check YOURSELF

Your party plans were complete, including all information and costs. You explained clearly in writing how multiplication and division were used in planning your party.

What are
the
chances?

What Are The Chances?

I win if the spin is an even number. You win if it is an odd number.

certain
not in a million years
for sure
likely
unlikely
probably
always
never
uncertain

I need a 12 to win.

It's Certainly Impossible

▶ Decide for each picture whether the given outcome is

CERTAIN

IMPOSSIBLE

LIKELY

UNLIKELY

UNCERTAIN

▶ Explain your reasoning.

TOMORROW IS TUESDAY

THE WEATHER WILL BE CLEAR AND COOL TOMORROW

TOMORROW IS DEC. 29

TOMORROW IS NEW YEAR'S EVE

ON YOUR OWN

1. How many reds do you think you would get in 100 spins? Why did you choose that number?

2. Draw a spinner that you are sure will always land on red.

3. Draw a spinner that will never land on red.

4. If you spin this spinner 100 times, about how many times do you think it will land on blue? About how many times on yellow?

5. Draw a spinner that you think will give 90 yellow and 10 red in 100 spins.

6. Draw a three-part spinner that you think will give 50 blue, 25 red, and 25 green in 100 spins.

7. *My Journal:* What did you learn that is new?

Chances Are

I wonder what the chances are that these flowers will grow?

I wonder if our team will win?

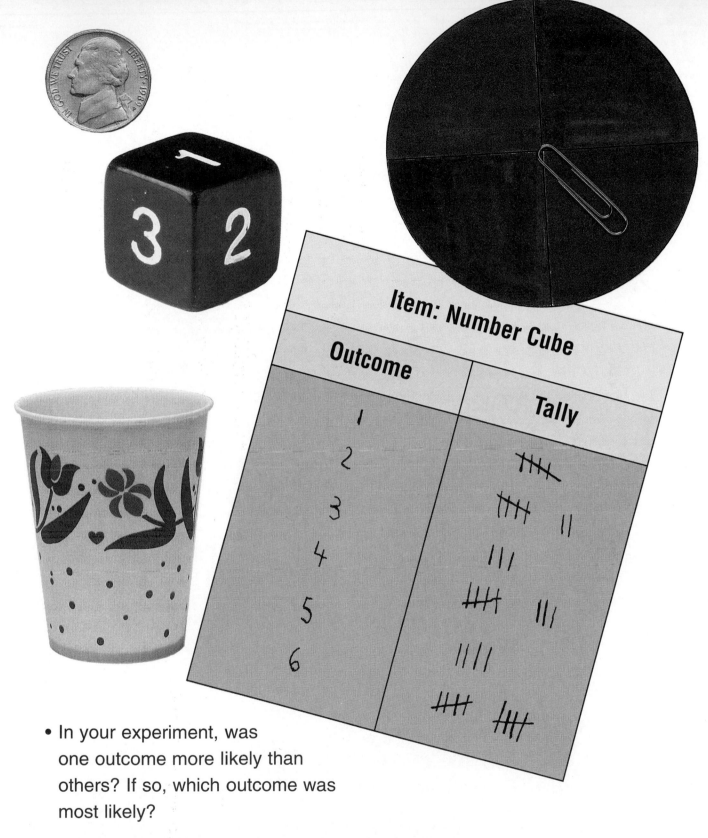

Item: Number Cube	
Outcome	Tally
1	
2	ЖЖ
3	ЖЖ II
4	III
5	ЖЖ III
6	IIII
	ЖЖ ЖЖ

- In your experiment, was one outcome more likely than others? If so, which outcome was most likely?

- Were your predictions close to the actual results of your experiment?

- Was it easy or difficult to make a prediction about your experiment? Why do you think this was so?

ON YOUR OWN

For each situation, write Yes if you think the outcomes are equally likely. Write No if you think they are not equally likely. Explain your reasoning.

1.

Outcomes	
Even Numbers	
Odd Numbers	

2.

Outcomes	
Heads	
Tails	

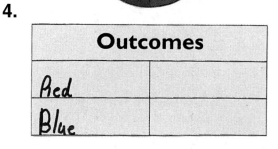

3.

Outcomes	
Red	
Blue	

4.

Outcomes	
Red	
Blue	

5. Describe one situation where you cannot predict the outcomes.

6. *My Journal:* Describe how you feel about chance. Give some examples of when your chances were "good."

What are the chances of landing in SOUTH AMERICA?

Have you ever wondered why South America looks so small on a flat map and looks so much larger on a globe?

Maps show the spherical or ball shape of the earth on a flat sheet of paper, but globes are similar in shape to the earth. They do not change a place's size.

Here is a way to show how flat maps change area.

Use a flat map of the earth and a globe. An inflatable globe ball would be ideal.

Put the flat map on a table or desk. Work with a partner. One person gently slides the map back and forth. The other drops a paper clip gently on the map about 100 times and records where it lands each time.

Then one person tosses the globe gently 100 times, catches it, and records where the right index finger hits.

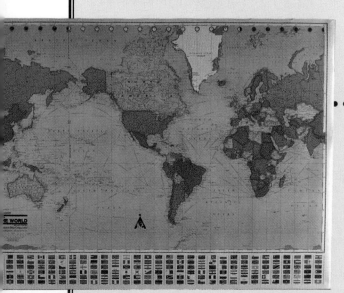

❶ Do you have a better chance of landing on South America on the globe or on the map?

❷ What can you conclude from your results?

THE
PROBABILITY
Game

Materials

Two spinners
Recording Sheets

Game Rules

1 Decide who will be Player A and who will be Player B.

2 Take turns spinning both spinners.

3 After spinning both spinners, add the numbers that come up.

4 Player A scores 1 point if the sum is either 2, 4, 6, or 8. Player B scores 1 point if the sum is either 3, 5, or 7.

5 First player with 10 points wins the round.

ON YOUR OWN

Think about each game. Then answer these questions:

• Is the game fair?

• If the game is not fair, which player do you think has a better chance of winning?

1. Toss two coins. Player A wins if both are either heads or tails. Player B wins if there is no match.

2. Spin the spinner twice. Player A wins if the two spins are the same color. Player B wins if the two spins are different colors.

3. Spin three times. Player A wins if any two spins match. Player B wins if all three spins are different.

4. Roll two 1-to-6 number cubes and add the faces. Player A wins if the sum is 7 or greater. Player B wins if the sum is less than 7.

5. *My Journal:* What do you think is important about making a game fair?

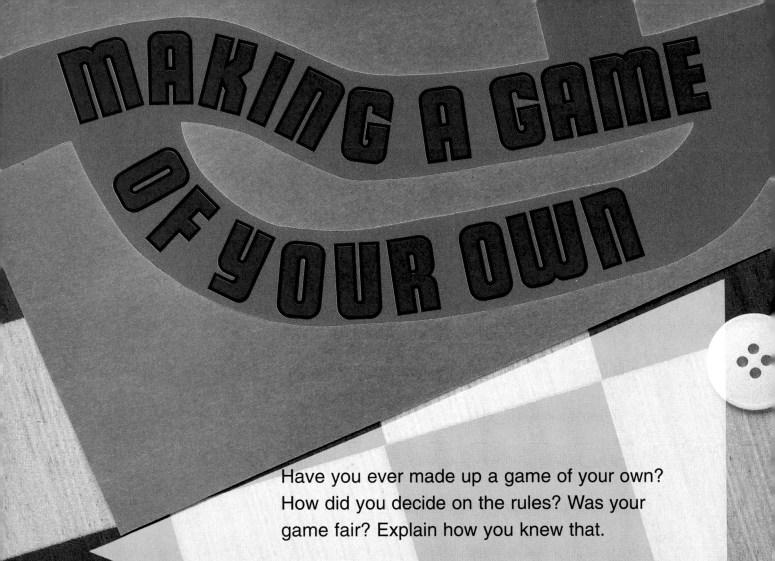

MAKING A GAME OF YOUR OWN

Have you ever made up a game of your own? How did you decide on the rules? Was your game fair? Explain how you knew that.

You will have a chance to make up a game of your own. Before you begin, warm up by writing some rules for the Four Colors Game.

THE FOUR COLORS GAME

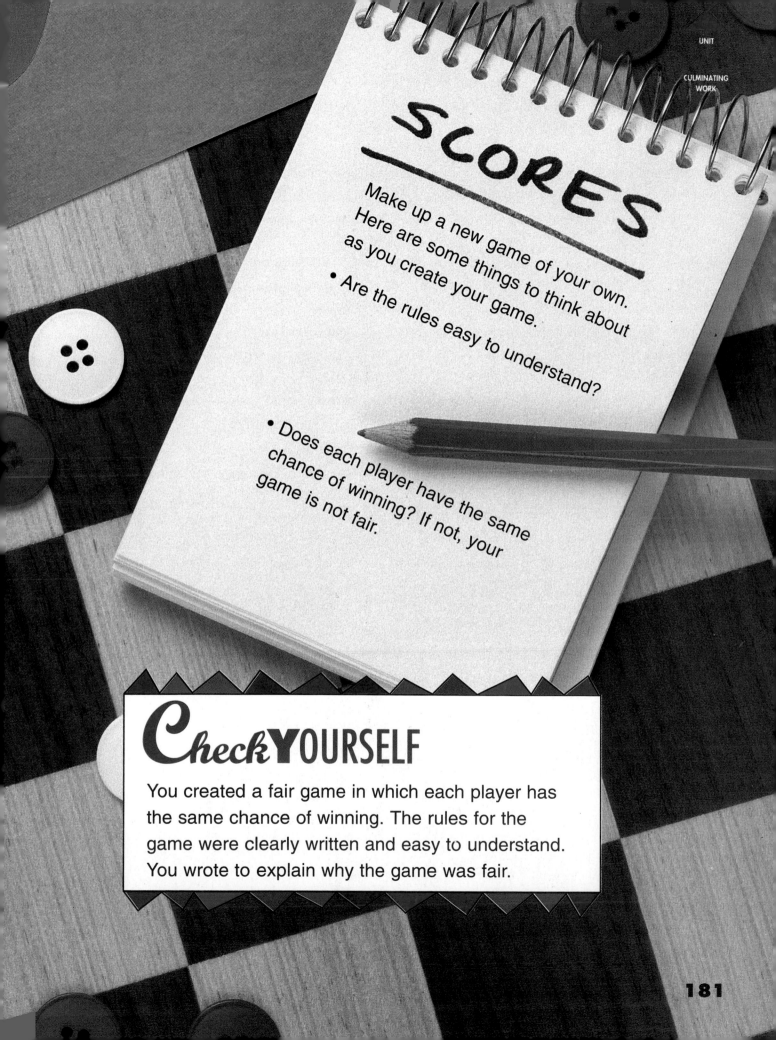

SCORES

Make up a new game of your own. Here are some things to think about as you create your game.

- Are the rules easy to understand?

- Does each player have the same chance of winning? If not, your game is not fair.

Check**YOURSELF**

You created a fair game in which each player has the same chance of winning. The rules for the game were clearly written and easy to understand. You wrote to explain why the game was fair.

Acknowledgments

ILLUSTRATION

Cover Illustration: **Seymour Chwast**
Victoria Allen: 24, 25, 68, 69; **Andrea Arroyo:** 82, 83; **Kevin Bapp:** 33; **George Baquero:** 114;
Jill Kagan Batelman: 84, 85; **Jennifer Bolten:** 118, 119; **Neverne Covington:** 30-32; **Janice Durand:** 178, 179;
Susan Foster: 88, 89; **Tara Framer:** 82, 92, 93, 131, 158-161; **Barbara Friedman:** 26, 27; **Tuko Fujisaki:** 42,
43; **Tom Gagliano:** 12, 13, 20, 21, 29, 63, 75, 76, 83, 129; **Pam-ela Harrelson:** 172, 173; **Susan Hartung:** 108,
141, 171, 174, 175; **Gary Johnson:** 9-11; **Tony Joyce:** 98; **Victoria Kann:** 132, 133;
Stanford Kay/Paragraphics: 4-6; **Kathleen Kinkopf:** 92, 93, 159-161; **Helen Kunze:** 146, 147;
Maria Pia Marella: 109, 110; **Claude Martinot:** 54, 55, 153, 154; **Mas Miyamoto:** 74, 124; **Cheryl Kirk Noll:**
155; **Julie Pace:** 8; **Robert Roper:** 60, 61, 172; **Marsha Serafin:** 100-102; **Neil Shigley:** 67; **Robert A. Soule:** 22,
23, 79, 80; **Michael Sours:** 86, 87; **George Ulrich:** 158; **Gregg Valley:** 90, 91; **K. Watt:** 131, 142, 143;
David Wink: 66.

PHOTOGRAPHY

Photo Management and Picture Research: **Omni-Photo Communications, Inc.**
Claire Aich: 24, 34, 35, 37, 56, 65, 72, 73, 75, 77, 78, 84, 85, 94, 95, 130, 147, 159, 168, 169, 180, 181;
©**Art Resource:** 111; ©**Hannah Baker/Bishop Museum:** 139; ©**Danilo Baschung/Leo DeWys, Inc.:** 38, 39;
©**Baum/Monkmeyer Press:** 13; **UPI/Bettman: 109;** ©**Bishop Museum:** 64; ©**Leslie Borden/Photo Edit:** 106,
107, 120, 121; ©**Robert Brenner:** 174; ©**Conklin/Monkmeyer Press:** 62; ©**Grace Davies/Omni-Photo
Communications:** 144; **Everett Studios:** 1, 16, 17, 58, 59, 70, 71, 96, 97, 104, 106, 107, 120, 121, 136, 137,
148-151, 166, 167; ©**Kenneth Fink/Photo Researchers:** 28; ©**Focus on Sports/Sixers vs Suns:** 128;
©**Fotopic/Omni-Photo Communications:** 174; ©**Tony Freeman/Photo Edit:** 3; ©**George F. Godfrey/Animals,
Animals:** 38; ©**The Granger Collection:** 3, 144; ©**Joel Greenstein/Omni-Photo Communications:** 65, 68;
Michael Groen: 122, 123, 134, 135; ©**Arron Haupt/Stock Boston:** 74; ©**Grant Heilman Photography:** 23;
Horizon: 115, 152; **Richard Hutchings:** 48, 103, 111, 177; ©**Richard Hutchings/Photo Researchers:** 138, 139;
Ken Karp: 2, 6, 13, 14, 98, 113, 140, 170, 171, 175, 176, 178; ©**Frans Lanting/Minden Pictures:** 81; **John Lei:**
i, 7, 30, 40, 42, 44, 82, 83, 99, 125-128, 130, 145; ©**John Lei/Omni-Photo Communications:** 18, 19, 36, 175,
176; ©**Erich Lessing/Art Resource:** 163; ©**Alexander Marshack:** 28, 29; ©**Meggett/Focus on Sports:** 128;
Monkmeyer Press: 62; ©**Nurisdany/Perennou/Science Source/Photo Researchers:** 15; ©**Raion
Oberlander/Stock Boston:** 144; **Steven Oglivy:** 2, 46, 49, 112, 116, 157; ©**Yoto Park/Omni-Photo
Communications:** 94; ©**Laurie Platte/Winfrey, Inc.:** 144; ©**M. Richards/Photo Edit:** 106, 107; ©**John M.
Roberts/The Stock Market:** 2; ©**Steve Ross/Leo DeWys, Inc.:** 18, 19; ©**Shelley Rotner/Omniphoto
Communications:** 170; ©**Nicolas Sapiena/Art Resource:** 138; ©**Earl Scott/Charles Eames:** 138; ©**John
Shaw/Tom Stack & Assoc.:** 139; ©**Dennis Stock/Magnum Photos:** 144; ©**Joseph Szkodzinski/The Image
Bank:** 144; ©**UPI/Bettman:** 114; ©**Steve Vidler/Leo DeWys, Inc.:** 138; ©**Marvin Wolf/Tony Stone Worldwide:**
140.

CALCULATORS

T-I 108
T-I Math Explorer

MANIPULATIVES

Link-Its ™
Power Polygons